ORTHO'S All About
Dry Climate
Gardening

Meredith® Books
Des Moines, Iowa

Ortho's All About Dry Climate Gardening
Editor: Denny Schrock
Writer: Gayle Weinstein
Contributing Technical Consultants: Elizabeth V. Gardener,
  Michael D. Smith, Douglas F. Welsh
Senior Associate Design Director: Tom Wegner
Assistant Editor: Harijs Priekulis
Copy Chief: Terri Fredrickson
Copy and Production Editor: Victoria Forlini
Editorial Operations Manager: Karen Schirm
Managers, Book Production: Pam Kvitne,
  Marjorie J. Schenkelberg, Rick von Holdt, Mark Weaver
Contributing Copy Editor: Lorraine Ferrell
Contributing Proofreaders: Becky Etchen, Jeanee Ledoux,
  Courtenay Wolf
Contributing Illustrator: Mike Eagleton
Contributing Map Illustrator: Jana Fothergill
Additional Contributor: Rosemary Kautzky
Indexer: Ann Truesdale
Editorial and Design Assistants: Kathleen Stevens,
  Karen McFadden

**Additional Editorial Contributions from
  Art Rep Services**
Director: Chip Nadeau
Designers: lk Design
Illustrators: Michael Surles, Shawn Wallace

Bittersweet Lane Publishing
Publishing Director: Michael MacCaskey

Meredith® Books
Editor in Chief: Linda Raglan Cunningham
Design Director: Matt Strelecki
Executive Editor, Gardening and Home Improvement:
  Benjamin W. Allen
Executive Editor, Gardening: Michael McKinley

Publisher: James D. Blume
Executive Director, Marketing: Jeffrey Myers
Executive Director, New Business Development:
  Todd M. Davis
Executive Director, Sales: Ken Zagor
Director, Operations: George A. Susral
Director, Production: Douglas M. Johnston
Business Director: Jim Leonard

Vice President and General Manager: Douglas J. Guendel

Meredith Publishing Group
President, Publishing Group: Stephen M. Lacy
Vice President-Publishing Director: Bob Mate

Meredith Corporation
Chairman and Chief Executive Officer: William T. Kerr

In Memoriam: E.T. Meredith III (1933–2003)

Note to the Readers: Due to differing conditions, tools,
and individual skills, Meredith Corporation assumes no
responsibility for any damages, injuries suffered, or losses
incurred as a result of following the information published
in this book. Before beginning any project, review the
instructions carefully, and if any doubts or questions remain,
consult local experts or authorities. Because codes and
regulations vary greatly, you always should check with
authorities to ensure that your project complies with all
applicable local codes and regulations. Always read and
observe all of the safety precautions provided by
manufacturers of any tools, equipment, or supplies,
and follow all accepted safety procedures.

Photographers
(Photographers credited may retain copyright ©
  to the listed photographs.)
L = Left, R = Right, C = Center, B = Bottom, T = Top

William D. Adams: 11B, 30, 73B, 85B; **Liz Ball/Positive
Images:** 73TR; **Patricia Bruno/Positive Images:** 37B, 56R;
Karen Bussolini/Positive Images: 65; **Brian Carter/
Garden Picture Library:** 63TL; **Christi Carter/Garden
Picture Library:** 60, 62L; **Kathy Adams Clark/KAC
Productions:** 85T, 90B, 107C; **Candace Cochran/Positive
Images:** 8BR; **R. Todd Davis:** 21C, 69B, 91, 121T; **Catriona
Tudor Erler:** 16T, 21TR, 25TR, 56L, 59; **Derek Fell:** 36T, 42,
44T, 52T, 79, 92B, 117T; **John Glover:** 5B, 83B; **Jessie M.
Harris:** 99T; **Saxon Holt:** 5T, 54T, 70T, 95T, 118T, 118C;
Bill Johnson: 101B, 105B, 106B, 107T, 115B, 116B;
Rosemary Kautzky: 20B, 25BR, 33B, 47B, 73TL, 97T;
Greg Lasley/KAC Productions: 8TL, 120B; **Charles Mann:**
1, 9L, 20T, 31, 54B, 70B, 71, 75, 87B, 89T, 89B, 93, 107B,
114T, 120T; **Clive Nichols:** 3T & 4 (Lady Farm, Somerset),
84TR; **Jerry Pavia:** 9R, 11TR, 12, 16B, 19B, 21TL, 48T, 53B,
58R, 68, 69TR, 72, 83T, 84TL, 88B, 106T, 109T, 111C, 111B,
113T; **Ben Phillips/Positive Images:** 66; **Cheryl R.
Richter:** 10, 77, 87T; **Richard Shiell:** 8TR, 8BL, 18L, 22,
41TR, 49, 63TR, 82T, 86T, 89C, 90T, 92T, 94B, 96C, 98T,
100T, 103T, 104B, 109B, 110B, 119; **J.S. Sira/Garden
Picture Library:** 81C; **Lauren Springer:** 103B; **Joseph G.
Strauch, Jr.:** 104T;
Jean Stutz: 31inset; **Michael S. Thompson:** 36B, 40T, 41TL,
41B, 43, 45, 48B, 53T, 53C, 55, 58L, 61, 62R, 69TL, 76, 78,
80, 81TL, 82B, 84B, 88T, 95B, 96T, 97B, 98B, 99B, 100B,
102B, 108B, 111T, 112, 113B, 114B, 116T; **Andy Wasowski:**
85C, 86B, 94T, 96B, 101T, 105T, 108T, 110T, 115T, 117B,
118B; **Rick Wetherbee:** 46, 63B, 81B; **David Winger:** 11TL,
18R, 21B, 64, 67, 74, 102T, 121B

Cover photograph: Charles Mann

All of us at Meredith® Books are dedicated to providing you
with the information and ideas you need to enhance your
home and garden. We welcome your comments and
suggestions about this book. Write to us at:
  Meredith Corporation
  Meredith Gardening Books
  1716 Locust St.
  Des Moines, IA 50309–3023

If you would like to purchase any of our gardening, home
improvement, cooking, crafts, or home decorating and
design books, check wherever quality books are sold.
Or visit us at: meredithbooks.com

If you would like more information on other Ortho
products, call 800/225-2883 or visit us at: www.ortho.com

Gardening in Dry Climates   4

Nature's Arid Environments   **5**
What Makes an Arid Environment?   **6**
Map of North American Arid Regions   **7**

Gardening Guidelines for Arid Regions   12

Growing Nonadapted Plants in Arid Regions   **14**
Making Use of Microclimates   **16**
Conserving with Microclimates   **20**

Fundamentals of Xeriscape Gardening   24

Know Your Soil   **24**
Soil Texture   **26**
Planting and Transplanting   **33**
Water and Xeriscaping   **36**
Managing for Water Conservation   **38**
Ways to Water   **40**
Fertilizers and Nutrition   **42**
Mulch   **45**
Pest Management   **48**

How to Xeriscape   50

Shaping a Xeriscape Garden   **51**
Conserving Resources   **55**
Creating Dry Gardens   **60**
Silver and Blue Gardens   **61**
Ornamental Grass Gardens   **64**
Sculpture Gardens   **68**
Prairie Gardens   **70**
Traditional Gardens Xeric Style   **76**
Victorian Gardens   **82**

Plants for Dry Climate Gardens   84

Selecting the Plant for the Site   **84**
Trees   **85**
Shrubs   **96**
Perennials   **108**

USDA Plant Hardiness Zone Map   **122**

Metric Conversions   **122**

Resources   **123**

Index   **124**

GARDENING IN
Dry Climates

Calamagrostis **'Karl Foerster' towers behind** *Rudbeckia,* *Echinacea,* **and white** *Liatris* **'Alba'.**

IN THIS CHAPTER

Nature's Arid Environments **5**

What Makes an Arid Environment? **6**

Map of North American Arid Regions **7**

Irrigated green lawns rimmed with shrubs and flowers mask the fact that most of western North America is arid. But when droughts hit and water supplies dwindle, residents remember the region's true climate. This book is about gardening in the arid West.

Somewhere between traditional gardening and the need to conserve our natural resources is xeriscaping. A xeriscape garden looks as beautiful as a traditional garden but uses far less water to maintain. The landscape contractors of Colorado and the Denver Water Department developed the xeriscape concept in 1981. Xeriscaping is "quality landscaping that conserves water and protects the environment" and involves seven basic principles:

■ Plan and design prior to planting
■ Analyze soil
■ Keep lawn size practical
■ Select appropriate plants
■ Irrigate efficiently
■ Use mulch
■ Maintain appropriately

Hundreds of years of gardening habits, often inherited from regions with abundant moisture, make gardening with less water seem challenging. You can, however, make many changes in your garden to conserve water and other resources. Sometimes merely working with microclimates, or slightly shifting gardening techniques makes a big difference. Growing less thirsty plants—and watering accordingly—can substantially change water needs.

Gardens and their plants thrive with less water when both are suited to their location and its conditions.

Xeriscaping is about choices that gardeners make every day and involve three major commitments:

BE CONSERVATIVE Use natural resources efficiently and wisely.

SEEK SUSTAINABILITY The less gardeners intervene, the fewer resources are consumed.

THINK ECOLOGICALLY Select and grow plants based on their relationships with

Creeping thyme softens the flagstone paving in this xeriscape garden, while blue salvia, pineleaf penstemon, yellow buckwheat, and pinks add texture and color.

Colorful catmint (foreground) and thyme (center) are plants that require relatively less water and contribute vigorous growth to dryland gardens.

the site, soil, and regional environment.

Xeriscaping is a practical choice, planned for the rigors of an arid climate that encourages gardeners to work with nature, not against it. This book is about how to manage your garden in an arid environment by using xeriscape principles and guidelines. Conservation is not just about saving water but also involves taking care of and protecting soil and minimizing potential soil and water pollutants.

Although written for arid western states, the concepts and guidelines are practical for gardening all over the world. As a gardener, you should become aware of the natural environment and resources available to you. Use nature as your guide by placing plants where they can thrive with minimal intervention. Let the site guide you in selecting plants that complement the space.

Nature's arid environments

Natural arid environments come in many forms: deserts, short- and mixed-grass prairies, shrublands, open woodlands, savannas, and parklands. Although these areas differ in topography, climate, vegetation, and wildlife, they have much in common. They have more sunny days than cloudy ones, generally receive less than 20 inches of rainfall a year, quickly lose moisture to evaporation, and experience high temperatures and low relative humidity. Because water is limited, soils create challenges as well (at least when gardening with traditional plants from humid environments). Arid-area soils are less worn and weathered, have minimal organic matter, and are more alkaline than soils in rainy areas.

What Makes an Arid Environment?

Imagine a desert—bright sunshine, hot temperatures, warm winds, little cloud cover, low relative humidity, and, most of all, little rain. It is water or lack of it in any form (rain, snow, fog, or dew) that creates the arid environment. Waters' scarcity becomes apparent in the vegetation prominent in deserts, short/mixed grass prairies, shrublands, savannas, and parklands.

Where are arid environments?

Arid environments occur where evaporation (from land and plants) is high and natural precipitation is low. This may happen as a result of one or more factors:

■ Where land is too far from an ocean (such as the Great Basin desert)
■ Where land is in the rain shadow of a mountain range (such as in the High Plains grassland)
■ Where descending air accelerates evaporation and precipitation is low and unpredictable (20 to 30 degrees north and south of the equator)
■ Where soil is unfavorable (heavy clay, coarse sand, saline soil, or shallow soil)
■ Where soil is unstable (sand dunes)

How do you garden in an arid environment?

Plants have evolved and adapted to their natural environments. Collectively, landforms and plants are the result of the growing conditions of the area, especially climate and soil. For example, deciduous forests emerge where there is adequate rainfall year round and where soil moisture is regularly replenished. Grasslands emerge where rainfall is adequate in spring but less so in hot summer months. Under these conditions, soil moisture is not deep and not recharged as often. Desert plants emerge when there is generally low, usually unpredictable rainfall. Soil moisture is shallow and rarely recharged. Because these arid environments and vegetative types indicate the resources they have for plants to grow and survive, you can look to them for clues on how and what to use in your garden. Xeriscape was first created in these latter regions. When you understand where you live and work in partnership with nature, you will be equipped to minimize your use of natural resources and be rewarded with a beautiful, productive, healthy garden.

Warm deserts

Deserts are replete with extremes and, because of this, difficult to define. Although noted for lack of rainfall—generally less than 10 inches per year—there are exceptions where some receive 20 inches per year. Deserts are not just affected by minimal rainfall, they are also influenced by when moisture comes and if it penetrates the soil.

Globally, most deserts occur at low latitudes and range from warm to hot.

Warm deserts experience very hot summers, little winter moisture, and occasional frosts. Hot deserts rarely experience frost. Cold deserts occur at higher latitudes or higher elevations. Winters there may be below freezing, and moisture can come in the form of snow.

Generally, deserts exhibit high daytime temperatures, often over 100° F. Because desert vegetation is scattered and doesn't cover the soil, the ground receives twice as much solar radiation as humid areas. On the other hand, deserts lose nearly twice as much heat at night as humid regions because there is no cloud cover (which results in a comfortable evening). In the desert, winds are drying, moisture evaporates quickly, and the soil remains dry. Sometimes rain may evaporate before reaching the ground. Soils are coarse or finely textured, alkaline, shallow, rocky, or gravelly with minimal or no organic matter. Although plants differ from one desert to the next, many have similar adaptive characteristics (see page 13). Deserts are truly nature's xeriscapes.

In the United States there are four major deserts: Chihuahuan, Sonoran, Mojave, and Great Basin. Each provides a wealth of inspiring ideas and plants for garden use. The Chihuahuan desert includes the southeastern portion of Arizona, much of New Mexico and Texas, as well as Mexico. El Paso, Texas, and Big Bend National Park are at its core; Albuquerque, New Mexico, borders its most northern tip. Here, summers are very hot and winters cool. The area receives an average of less than 10 inches of rain per year, mostly in the summer. Many attractive shrubs and small trees from this desert provide versatile

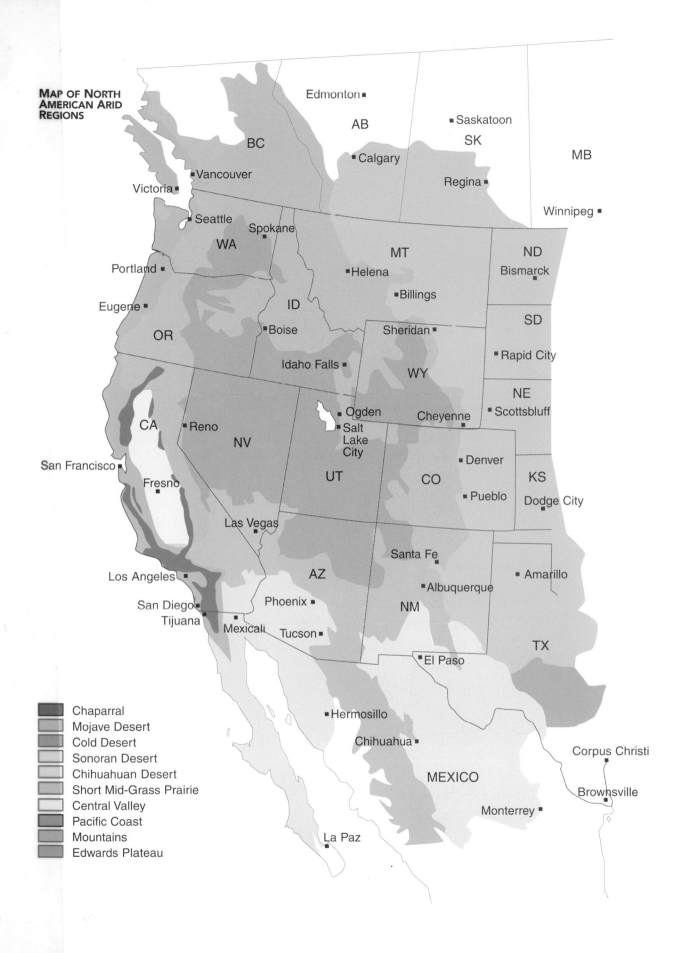

MAP OF NORTH AMERICAN ARID REGIONS

Edmonton ■

■ Saskatoon

AB

SK

MB

■ Calgary

Regina ■

BC

Vancouver ■

Victoria ■

Seattle ■

Spokane ■

WA

MT

ND

Bismarck ■

Helena ■

Portland ■

ID

■ Billings

Eugene ■

SD

■ Boise

Sheridan ■

OR

Idaho Falls ■

■ Rapid City

WY

NE

Ogden ■

Scottsbluff ■

CA

■ Reno

■ Salt Lake City

Cheyenne ■

NV

■ Denver

San Francisco ■

UT

CO

KS

Fresno ■

■ Pueblo

Dodge City ■

Las Vegas ■

Santa Fe ■

■ Amarillo

AZ

Albuquerque ■

Los Angeles ■

Phoenix ■

NM

San Diego ■

Tijuana ■

Mexicali ■

Tucson ■

TX

El Paso ■

■ Winnipeg

Hermosillo ■

Corpus Christi

Chihuahua ■

MEXICO

Brownsville ■

Monterrey ■

La Paz ■

■ Chaparral
■ Mojave Desert
■ Cold Desert
■ Sonoran Desert
■ Chihuahuan Desert
■ Short Mid-Grass Prairie
■ Central Valley
■ Pacific Coast
■ Mountains
■ Edwards Plateau

What Makes an Arid Environment?
continued

The Joshua tree, the indicator plant of the Mojave desert, is an excellent accent for that arid desert region. *Right:* Many desert plants, such as these cacti, adapt readily to gardens.

choices for dry gardens; for example, agave, Apache plume, desert willow, honey mesquite, mescal bean, Mormon-tea, western soapberry, and white thorn acacia.

The Sonoran desert includes southwestern Arizona, southeastern California, most of Baja California, and the western half of Sonora, Mexico. Well-known cities of this desert (thanks to irrigation) are Palm Springs, California, and Tucson and Phoenix, Arizona. Although this is a very hot desert, it has periods of rain in winter and summer. The saguaro cactus is its hallmark. The Sonoran desert is diverse with annuals, shrubs, and trees. You can choose from desert marigold, poppies and lupines, jojoba, ironwood, saltbush, and mesquites. Along streamsides in Arizona are ash, black walnut, cottonwood, and willow trees.

The Mojave desert lies north of the Sonoran desert in southeastern California,

and much of Nevada, Arizona, and Utah at elevations between 2,000 and 5,000 feet. Summers are hot, dry, and windy. Although winters are relatively mild, temperatures may fall below freezing. This arid environment receives less than 5 inches of mostly winter rainfall. Barstow, California, and Las Vegas, Nevada, are populated areas in this desert. The Joshua tree, the hallmark plant of this area, is found primarily at higher elevation. This desert extends below sea level in Death Valley. Other plants include big sagebrush, blackbush, bursage, catclaw acacia, creosote bush, mesquite, and shadscale.

Living in warm deserts means numerous possibilities for creating textural and sculptured gardens composed of the most artful plants.

Cold deserts

In North America, the only major cold desert is the Great Basin. Sandwiched between the Rocky Mountains and Sierra Nevada ranges, it reaches British Columbia, Canada, and includes portions of Oregon, Idaho, California, Utah, Nevada, and Wyoming. Some place the Four Corners region of Utah, Colorado, and New Mexico into the Great Basin region. Cities include Salt Lake City, Utah; Reno, Nevada; and Boise and Twin Falls, Idaho.

The Great Basin cold desert, above and right, introduces a variety of silver and gray foliage plants adapted to harsh, dry conditions.

Purple prairie clover is just one of many wildflowers found in short-and mixed-grass prairies.

Grasslands vary from short to mixed to tallgrass prairies, depending on moisture and soil. This one includes *Rudbeckia hirta*, *Echinacea purpurea*, and *Dalea purpurea*.

Because of its more northerly latitude and higher elevations (3,000 to 6,500 feet), the Great Basin is considered a cold desert. Annual precipitation is 7 to 12 inches a year, evenly distributed throughout the year. Winter low temperatures are below freezing; precipitation often falls as snow. Like the Chihuahuan desert, the Great Basin is also considered a shrub desert with sagebrush as its hallmark. Other plants include blackbrush, desert globe mallow, greasewood, Mormon tea, prickly poppy, saltbush, snakeweed, and yellow bee plant.

A cold desert provides opportunities to use silver and gray foliage plants with the pinks, yellows, and whites found in the rock formations.

Grasslands

Like deserts, grasslands vary in types and environments. Unlike deserts, their dominant cover is grass. In grasslands, trees are generally absent except along waterways. Although these areas appear flat, they are often rolling with gentle swales and steep hillsides where shrubs or trees usually grow.

Globally, grasslands are found in semiarid, continental climates of middle latitudes. They experience many sunny days, a wide range in daily and seasonal temperatures, strong drying winds, and high evaporation. They typically receive 10 to 20 inches of rain a year, much falling in spring as snow. Winters are cold, summers are warm to hot. Winter snow often blows into drifts, leaving vegetation exposed and unprotected from the cold. Annual rainfall and soil influence the plant species and height of grassland vegetation. Tall grass prairies (not included in semiarid environments) are found where precipitation is more than 20 inches a year. These areas have rich, fertile soil with grasses ranging 4 to 10 feet tall. Short-grass prairies (8 to 18 inches tall) generally receive less than 15 inches a year. In some areas rainfall can be as low as 8 inches. Soils are moderate to low in organic matter. Water penetration is not deep, and salts often accumulate. Mixed-grass prairie (1½ to 4 feet tall) is a combination of short and moderately tall grasses usually found in areas with less than 20 inches of precipitation.

The major grassland in North America is in the Great Plains. Centrally located between the deciduous forest in the East to the base of the Rocky Mountains in the West, it stretches north into Canada and south into Central Mexico. As moisture decreases from east to west, grass height and species change near the 98th meridian from the tall-grass prairie that borders the eastern forest to short-grass prairie. Cities in the semiarid grasslands include Denver, Colorado; Billings, Montana; and Tulsa, Oklahoma.

Trees typically found along waterways in the short- and mixed-grass prairies include cottonwoods, alders, birch, and willows. Grasses include needlegrass, blue grama, buffalo grass, galleta grass, little bluestem, and western wheatgrass. Wildflowers include asters, blazing stars, coneflowers, evening primroses, globe mallows, goldenrods, penstemons, sunflowers, and wild indigos, among many others.

A semiarid grassland environment provides the opportunity to create harmonious meadows with the subtle details in color and form usually found in nature.

What Makes an Arid Environment?
continued

Texas Canyon in the Dragoon Mountains east of Tucson is filled with live oak, manzanita, agave, grasses, and wildlife.

Shrublands

Shrublands provide a variety of species well-adapted as windbreaks, living barriers, and hedges. These specimens provide strong contrast between the foliage and bark, the branching structure and overall form, and the texture and growth habit.

Shrubs are plants with several woody stems at or near their base. They may be 1 to 15 feet high. Some shrubs grow in thickets where branches and roots interlock; others are found in scattered groups. Many can be trained as small single or multi-stem trees. Where land is arid, shrubs are smaller and more widely spaced with grass or bare ground beneath. Shrubland vegetation usually represents some seasonal weather variation such as moist winters and dry summers.

Shrublands are not usually recognized as major vegetative communities, although they predominate in deserts and chaparral. They grow in many arid environments:

■ Areas with dry slopes and foothills in western mountain ranges where soil is gravelly;

■ Areas adjacent to open woodlands where annual precipitation is low and evaporation high;

■ Wherever conditions are unsuitable for trees and grasses;

■ Where wind and temperature limit moisture uptake and prevent tree establishment. The amount and type of precipitation, sunlight, seasonal variation, and temperature determine the shrub's status.

Four general types of arid shrublands include chaparral, soft chaparral, semiarid scrub, and thornscrub.

CHAPARRAL is a community of plants that grows in Mediterranean climates with wet winters and dry summers. In the United States, they are found on arid slopes of western mountain ranges and in some desert environments. Chaparral plants are diverse and well-suited to thrive in drought conditions. They range in height from 3 to 12 feet and are densely branched with rigid stems and small, thick evergreen leaves. Individually, some make excellent ornamental plants. Many can be trained as small trees. In a group they can provide a coarse, textured barrier or hedge. Chaparral plants include shrubby evergreen oak, manzanita, ceanothus, and evergreen sumac. Though specific plants differ, cities as diverse as Santa Barbara, California, and Sedona, Arizona, have chaparral plants.

Soft chaparral consists mainly of plants that have soft, hairy leaves with less rigid branch structure. They intermingle with hard chaparral or grow on dry, rocky, south-facing slopes, gradually becoming more dominant at lower elevations. In many areas, these shrubs are widely spaced with nonwoody plants beneath them.

SAGEBRUSH is the most common soft chaparral shrub. Others include culinary herbs from the Mediterranean, such as sage, rosemary, thyme, and oregano. Soft chaparral plants are commonly found growing with the more familiar hard chaparral or grow below them at lower elevations. Many attractive garden plants are soft chaparral.

SEMIARID SCRUB grows in areas where winter temperatures are more severe; deciduous plants take the place of evergreen chaparral. Shrublands become deciduous. Plants found in this environment include Gambel oak, mountain mahogany, New Mexican locust, serviceberry, and sumac. This vegetation is common in the foothills of western mountain ranges where winter temperatures are frequently below freezing.

THORNSCRUB is the other common community of shrubland plants. Although primarily from the tropics, thornscrub has dispersed northward into drier areas at lower elevations where rainfall is less than 15 to 20 inches per

Various chaparral plants are found in Oak Creek Canyon in the Coconino National Forest near Sedona, Arizona.

American plum (*Prunus americana*) can create an excellent natural barrier.

High mountain meadows resemble those at lower elevations, but the plants often differ.

year. It occurs in warm deserts and consists of many mixed thorny shrubs, small trees, and columnar cacti, such as the cardon and organ pipe cactus. The latter rise above the thornscrub canopy, making these plant groups easier to spot. Feature plants include mesquite, palo verde, acacias, among others from the more southern parts of the Sonoran and Chihuahuan deserts.

Open woodlands

Open woodlands, found in California's foothills, are different from true forests. Although they consist of trees, the trees are smaller, more spread apart, and sometimes shrublike. Such woodlands are sometimes called "pygmy forests." Woodlands are transitional communities found between desert shrublands and mountainous forests. They often inhabit steep slopes where the soil is gravelly with little organic matter. Annual precipitation is 10 to 15 inches per year. Plant species in these communities have evolved with drought and cold temperatures.

Dominant plants include piñon pine, juniper, cypress, shrub oaks, mountain mahogany, and yuccas along with herbaceous buckwheat, evening primrose, and morning glory. Piñons tend to dominate at higher elevations and form more closed canopies similar to a forest. Junipers grow at lower elevations in more arid areas.

Open woodlands foster development of winter garden ideas and illustrate various combinations of plants just right for spot gardens.

Savannas and parklands

Savannas and parklands are communities of scattered trees with an under cover of grass dotted with wildflowers. Savannas—picture central Texas or California's Central Valley—are composed of broadleaf trees (deciduous or evergreen). Parklands are composed of needle evergreens. West of Denver, Colorado, in the foothills of the Rocky Mountains, are typical parklands. Trees are scattered and do not provide a closed canopy as in a forest. This allows grasses and wildflowers to receive sufficient sunlight for full development. Savannas and parklands develop in areas where there is seasonal moisture and drought. Lack of precipitation (savannas) or poor soil conditions (parklands) may cause dry soil conditions. Plants include Rocky Mountain juniper, ponderosa pine, bur oak, live oak, grasses and wildflowers. These semiarid landscapes are compelling because they unify grasses and trees in a water-conserving alliance. Many common urban and suburban gardens create artificial savannas and parklands. Instead of watering the lawn to keep it green in the dry season, allow it to go dormant. The dark green foliage of live oak, pine, or juniper against a background of golden-brown, grassy foliage is as striking in a garden as it is in nature. Both savannas and parklands provide excellent wildlife habitat.

High mountain meadows resemble those at lower elevations, but the plants often differ.

Savannas, such as this California hillside, are areas of scattered trees with an understory of grasses and wildflowers.

GARDENING GUIDELINES FOR
Arid Regions

If you live in an area once a prairie, choose garden plants from a prairie environment.

IN THIS CHAPTER

Growing
Nonadapted Plants
in Arid Regions **14**

Making Use of
Microclimates **16**

Conserving with
Microclimates **20**

Your goal is a garden with adapted and thriving plants, because the most rewarding xeric garden is one where plants flourish with minimal care.

Plants in arid environments adapt various mechanisms to survive. Although they use water the same as other plants, they retain it differently. Plants suited to arid environments are not necessarily growing in unsuitable conditions; they have evolved and adapted to these conditions. And their survival is not necessarily about minimal amounts of water. Their survival is about how they survive with less.

Plants are able to grow and reproduce because they have developed mechanisms over time, enabling them to use what is available. For example, cacti have root systems near the surface capable of capturing small amounts of moisture. They also have succulent stems that retain moisture for hard times. Many soft-stemmed plants have hairy or waxy leaves that minimize water loss. Some trees and shrubs drop their leaves to reduce water loss and depend on their green stems for photosynthesis. Many grasses roll their blades inward to minimize transpiration. Other plants have extensive or deep root systems capable of exploring large volumes of soil. Some plants propagate vegetatively so that in dry years, when fruits or seeds cannot

develop, they can still reproduce. Still others produce underground stems in shifting sand, to adapt to specific soil types. Through these and many other responses, plants have tuned into arid environments.

Growing natives or adapted exotic plants in arid regions

Gardeners, too, can tune in to arid environments and have more with less. A plant's water need is based on what it takes to keep it alive and healthy. To survive, a desert plant may require only two-thirds the water a grassland plant needs, and less than one-third the water a plant from a humid region needs.

GARDENING GUIDELINES

- Grow native or adapted plants. If growing adapted plants, choose those from environments similar to your region.
- Group plants with similar water needs.
- Plan the garden to fit the site. Work with the site as it is, using the existing features and microclimates.
- Note how water moves on the site.
- Get to know the soil.
- Keep resources on site.
- Use resources wisely.
- Reuse and recycle.

To grow plants with minimal water, you must select the appropriate plant for the site. The following tips are strategies that will help you benefit the most when growing plants that are adapted to arid environments.

SELECT PLANTS that come from areas similar to your region. If you live in a city that was once a cold desert, select plants that naturally come from a cold desert. If you live in an area that was once short-grass prairie, select plants that naturally grow in a prairie environment.

CHOOSE PLANTS SIMILAR TO YOUR ENVIRONMENT: Selecting plants from similar environments provides you with many choices as long as the plants do not have invasive tendencies. (Many cultivated plants are classified as noxious weeds because they crowd out surrounding native species.)

Where possible, choose plants native to your area since they have evolved with the climate and are not legally noxious (even if somewhat aggressive). Consult your state agricultural agency for a list of noxious weeds.

ALWAYS GROUP PLANTS WITH SIMILAR WATER NEEDS: If you grow desert and prairie plants in the same bed, you will have to water for plants with the highest need. This is not an effective use of water. Know your site and its microclimates and select appropriate plants for your property.

Plants adapted to arid environments generally grow slower than plants from humid environments and need less water. However, newly planted plants need water until they become established.

DRY CLIMATE LEAF ADAPTATIONS

Small narrow foliage: Fourwing saltbush

Scale-like foliage: Rocky Mountain juniper

Thick, leathery foliage: Greenleaf manzanita

Hairy foliage: Lamb's-ears

Succulent, fleshy foliage: Echeveria

Spiney leaves: Barrel cactus

DRY CLIMATE STEM ADAPTATIONS

Swollen stem: Kedrostis

Bulb: Sea onion

Succulent stem: Prickly pear cactus

DRY CLIMATE ROOT ADAPTATIONS

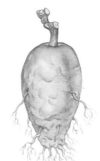
Thickened root: Night-blooming cereus

Succulent root: Oxalis

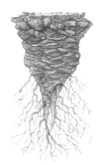
Swollen root: Hardy gloxinia

Growing Nonadapted Plants in Arid Regions

Growing nonadapted plants—those from more humid areas—in an arid environment is challenging but still possible. The goal is to minimize the use of water and other natural resources as much as possible. Consider the following guidelines as you develop or retrofit your garden to xeriscaping.

MAKE THE GARDEN FIT THE SITE: Plan the garden to fit the site rather than fitting the site to the garden. Planning the garden to fit the site involves two processes: working with the site as it is and making use of microclimates.

WORK WITH THE SITE AS IT IS: Before you disrupt the site, move or amend the soil, first consider the character and resources that already exist on your property. Moving or disrupting soil can change its structure, disturb microorganisms, increase soil evaporation, damage existing plant roots, and even change drainage patterns.

NOTE HOW WATER MOVES: Observe the site and watch how rain, snowmelt, or irrigation water moves on your property. You may be able to take advantage of water flows and use the existing contours of the land when you plant. Note drainage patterns from adjacent sites. Sometimes these provide additional water for plants.

EXAMINE SOIL TYPES: Consider whether the soil needs amending and whether the plants you would like to grow are suitable for the existing soil.

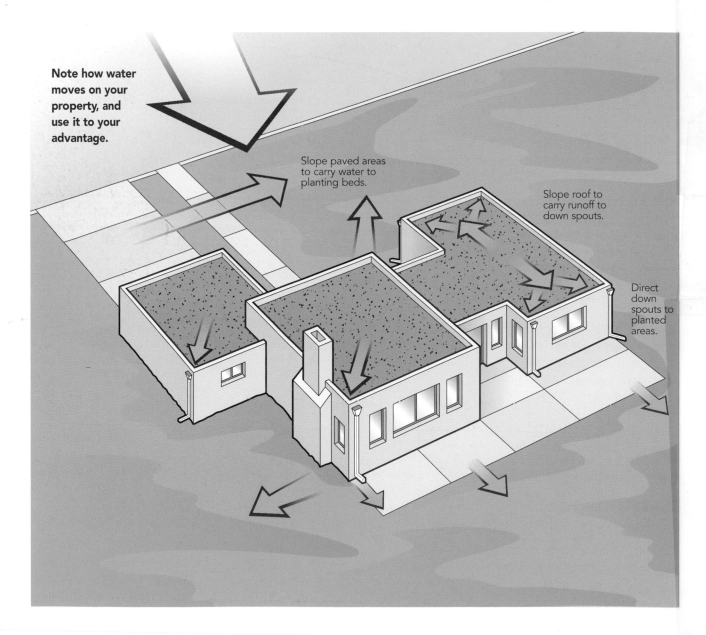

Note how water moves on your property, and use it to your advantage.

Slope paved areas to carry water to planting beds.

Slope roof to carry runoff to down spouts.

Direct down spouts to planted areas.

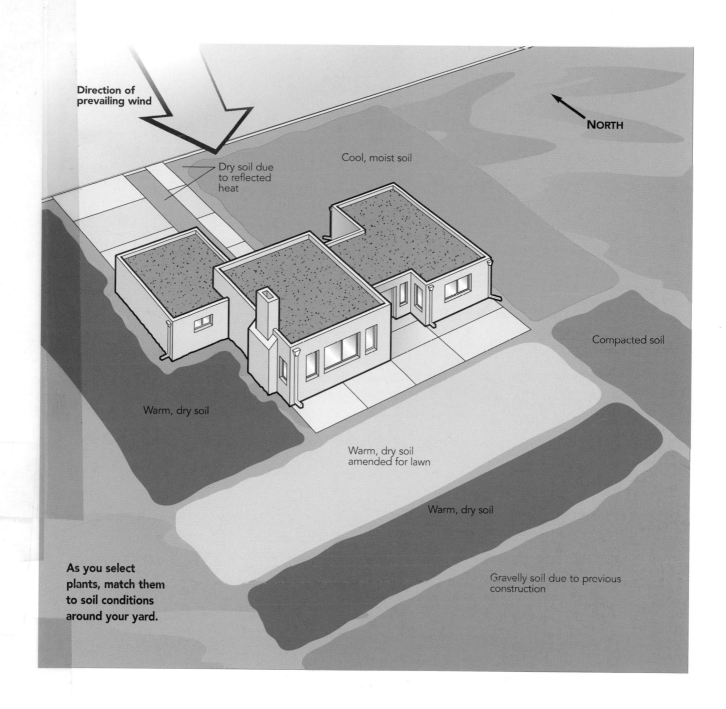

Direction of prevailing wind

NORTH

Dry soil due to reflected heat

Cool, moist soil

Compacted soil

Warm, dry soil

Warm, dry soil amended for lawn

Warm, dry soil

Gravelly soil due to previous construction

As you select plants, match them to soil conditions around your yard.

All types of plantings

You should pursue some aspects of gardening regardless of the type of plants you use.

USE EXISTING FEATURES:

Rock outcroppings or other unique features can create a special microclimate.

PROTECT NATIVE VEGETATION:

Locate native plants on sites where portions of the natural environment remain intact.

KEEP RESOURCES ON-SITE:

Use valuable resource materials such as leaf litter or grass clippings as mulch or as a soil amendment.

EVALUATE YOUR GARDEN:

Walk around the entire site with conservation in mind. Determine which plants are worth keeping and discard those that consume much and give back little.

Making Use of Microclimates

Microclimates are mini environments around your plants, house, fence, walls, and other structures. They can be sunny, shady, windy, wet, moist, or dry places. Each provides an opportunity to garden in a different way; each has advantages and disadvantages. Once you know the range of growing conditions on your property, you can choose how best to use them and what plants will be most suitable for the site.

Plants chosen to match microclimates are healthier, easier to maintain and require less water.

South-facing slopes receive the full brunt of sun and heat. Adjust your plant choice and maintenance accordingly.

Microclimates and sun

Silver-blue plants like these are adapted to intense sunlight.

South-facing areas including level ground, vertical walls, slopes, terraces, and raised beds receive full sun and are exposed to more heat. As a consequence, the soil is warmer and dries out more quickly. By contrast, north-facing areas are usually in shade most of the day and have cooler conditions very different from the south side. For example, a north side of a building in shade and a south side of a building in sun may have a temperature difference at noon between 10° and 15° F. The south side is the environment for plants that prefer full sun, tolerate heat, and grow in dry soil. On the north side, you can grow plants like understory plants that prefer shade. You can also grow plants that do best in cooler soil and rely on dependable moisture, such as those from more humid environments. Be aware that in winter, north exposures may also be subjected to desiccating winds. Watch nonadapted plants more closely for dryness, especially if you do not modify the wind pattern.

West-facing exposures are shady in the morning but receive afternoon sun and warm temperatures in summer. Unless you are growing plants that are adapted to these conditions, plants will need regular watering in summer because they may also be subjected to hot, drying winds.

East-facing exposures receive full morning sun and shade during the hottest part of the day. Because of this, temperatures are more moderate than south and west exposures. East exposures are also more protected from drying winds. Here you can grow plants that require more gentle sun but flourish with some shade.

Microclimates and wind

Wind tunnels develop in a garden when structures or

Labels on image (clockwise from top right): Full shade, Partial shade, Variable shade, Controlled shade, Full sun, Morning sun, Controlled shade, Warm and sunny

The temperature difference between the north and south sides of buildings can be 10 to 15° F, creating varied microclimates.

trees force the wind through narrow spaces. Strong winds can be very damaging to plants not only because they cause breakage but also because they remove moisture from the soil and from the plants. In winter, windy sites are especially detrimental to broadleaf evergreens from more humid regions. To curb the winds, you can plant a windbreak of tolerant plants to act as a filter, not a barrier, to reduce the airflow. You can also group deciduous plants close together. This increases humidity and reduces evaporation. Winds are also damaging when they come from the coast. They may carry salt injurious to plants. This is one environment where growing adapted plants is most critical.

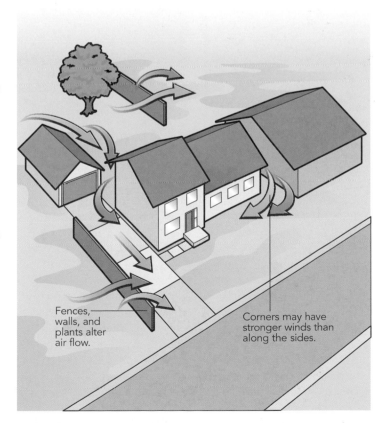

Fences, walls, and plants alter air flow.

Corners may have stronger winds than along the sides.

Strong winds remove moisture from plants and soil. Deflecting the wind can reduce evaporation.

Making Use of Microclimates
continued

Black holes, such as areas under the eaves, are garden beds that are sheltered from rain.

Shade cast by these aspens is dappled, and their roots compete aggressively for available moisture.

Microclimates and shade

Shade is found under tree canopies, near buildings and overhangs, and on north exposures.

Shaded areas can be moist or dry. Dry shade often occurs where plants are growing under the shade of trees. Here they compete with the tree roots for nutrients and moisture, especially shallow-rooted trees. Roots competing for limited surface water cause soil to dry out more quickly. Unless the shade-tolerant plants are adapted to low moisture, the area will require regular watering during the growing season.

Dry shade may also occur near walls or fences or under eaves where these structures obstruct or block natural precipitation. These areas are sometimes referred to as "black holes." Black holes are difficult because they generally do not receive any natural precipitation and are easily forgotten. Although many plants tolerate dry shade, they are totally dependent on irrigation under these conditions.

Microclimates and slopes

Slopes may have different soil characteristics from top to bottom. At the top and along the slopes, the soil may be drier because it drains quickly and holds less moisture. The steeper the slope, the drier the soil. At the base, the soil retains more moisture and may have more nutrients. The slope of the land also affects sunlight. Slopes tend to be warmer and sunnier on the south, whereas they may be shady, cool, and damp year-round on the north side.

Microclimates and hard surfaces

Asphalt, concrete, brick, or stone-paved areas such as patios, driveways, and sidewalks absorb and radiate heat. These elements change normal conditions. Light surface materials like marble or rock reflect light. These

Reduce glare and heat by using plants to create filtered shade.

conditions speed evaporation and transpiration on nearby soil and plants. You can modify patio surfaces by interplanting stone or brick with low-growing shrubs or ground covers such as thyme, wooly veronica, or pussy-toes. The combination of plants and stone increases humidity. Roots under the shade of the paving materials are in cooler, moister environments that make a more suitable growing site. You can also reduce glare by using warmer colors or creating shade with trees, shrubs, vines, laths, and arbors.

Modify hard surfaces by interrupting the areas with low-growing plants.

Conserving with Microclimates

Use a sprawling woody plant with a crown outside the black hole, where it can receive natural precipitation.

Conserving resources is important to xeriscaping. You can begin by selecting plants adapted to your site and carefully matching plants to the microclimates in your garden. However, once you meet these goals, you are now challenged to grow healthy plants by conserving resources. Locating the right plant for these different growing conditions can make a difference in plant growth and maintenance. Even rocks can provide microclimates for small plants. Knowing which site in arid areas offers the most protection from hot sun and dry winds will enable you to grow plants normally adapted to cooler climates. You can reduce some water use by mulching the soil, using drip irrigation, and creating filtered or partial shade to temper the heat. Less heat, more shade and more wind protection, and appropriate plant placement will save water in your garden, especially with nonadapted plants. Otherwise, you will need to apply water regularly.

Use resources wisely

Apply gardening techniques that will conserve water and save natural resources. New garden technologies such as drip and sub-surface irrigation continually become more practical and convenient. Soil moisture sensors are now available to take the guess-work out of knowing when to water (see page 36).

You can lessen water loss by proven techniques such as grouping plants to raise relative humidity, layering plants to create shade, or mulching soil to reduce weed competition and decrease evaporation.

Other techniques involve checking plant growth and water needs. Apply water only when needed and provide only as much water as necessary.

Take advantage of natural precipitation by timing planting or transplanting activities prior to anticipated natural precipitation whenever possible. Watering efficiently is based on the natural plant-growth cycle. For example, cool-season plants grow in spring and fall and go dormant in summer. Warm-season plants grow in summer and are dormant from mid-fall

Drip irrigation is the more efficient way to water this narrow bed.

Match irrigation techniques with bed shape by using drip or bubbler irrigation.

Be creative: Avoid planting where growing conditions are extremely difficult, as in this rock outcropping.

This slope with prickly pear cactus is covered by annual lupine.

through mid-spring. Apply the minimum water needed to maintain the plant in an acceptable condition during its growing season and allow it to go dormant when it naturally does. Plants generally do not need applied water when dormant, but do when growing under extreme stress. Apply water only to make up for lack of natural precipitation.

Garden to keep your plants healthy but not growing so fast that they require frequent pruning. Because water is a growth regulator, minimize what you provide. If a plant puts on abundant new growth, reduce the water. Pruning stimulates growth and requires more water. Keep plants in their natural form and prune only when necessary.

Do not push excess plant growth with fertilizers. Rapidly growing plants will require more water to support their growth. Fertilize instead to maintain plant health. Amend the soil not as a matter of routine but only as needed (see page 42).

Minimize the use of and need for resources

If growth rate is important such as with lawns, reduce the lawn size to only what you need. If the lawn is subject to high use, then keep it actively growing. If it is decoration, let it go dormant. Place and group plants with the highest water needs where the soil is cooler and retains the most moisture. Place those with the lowest water needs where the soil is warmer and drains quickly. If water is available at more depth, select plants that develop deep root systems.

Locate nonadapted plants away from the prevailing winds. Provide partial shade with plants or structures such as lath. Shade can cool temperatures 10° to 20° F and thus reduce water loss. Shade hard surfaces of brick, concrete, or asphalt to keep radiated heat from increasing temperatures and evaporation in adjacent garden areas.

Avoid creating planting beds that are difficult to water, such as areas with acute angles or beds that are narrow.

A still-dormant warm-season lawn of buffalograss is graced by blooming crocus, a cool-season bloomer.

Conserving with Microclimates
continued

Replace lawn with plants requiring little water. This is sun rose (*Helianthemum*) and Jupiter's beard (*Centranthus*) under a canopy of blue oak trees.

Where appropriate, avoid plants requiring high water use. Replace cool-season lawns with warm-season grass or substitute lawns with other ground covers.

Plant according to soil type and amend the soil only when it will improve growing conditions and water retention for the particular plant. Plants from humid environments do best in garden loam. If you live in an arid environment, your soil may need improvement. Plants from arid environments, however, do not always need amended soil as long as the existing soil drains well.

Find opportunities to use plants to improve soil. Grow nitrogen-fixing plants in sandy soil, eliminating the need for fertilizer. Most importantly, do not use materials (such as mountain peat moss) that destroy natural ecosystems somewhere else (see soil amendment, page 30).

Use plants that are best adapted to average natural rainfall patterns. Based on this, decide how much you are willing to irrigate. Then develop water-use zones by creating an overall water availability map of your property. This should include water from adjacent sites and water you can apply. (See pages 38 and 39.)

Avoid water waste by eliminating steep berms and slopes because water runs off too quickly. If this is not possible, direct the runoff to other sites in the garden, or terrace the slope or berm.

Do not plant in "black holes," those few locations around most houses that rain never reaches, such as under eaves. The plant you place in this location will always be dependent on irrigation.

Recycle available resources by shredding and applying collected leaves to a perennial garden.

Reuse and recycle materials whenever possible

Eliminate the demand for resources by recycling and reusing materials on your site.

If you compost all plant debris and kitchen wastes, you can use this compost as a soil amendment or as mulch. By allowing leaf litter to remain under trees and shrubs, you minimize weed competition and reduce evaporation (see page 42).

You often lose water because of runoff from natural rain or from irrigation. Harvest this runoff by capturing and directing it to garden sites requiring more moisture. You can collect rainwater from gutters and hold it for later use, but be sure to check with local codes before setting up such a system.

PLANT BY SOIL TYPE AND WATER USE

Chaparral plants often grow in gravelly soil.
Mid-grass prairie plants often grow in sandy soil.
Succulent plants often grow in granitic soil.
Short-grass prairie plants often grow in clay soil.
Plants from humid environments do best in loam.

FUNDAMENTALS OF
Xeriscape Gardening

To minimize water loss, plant in the coolest part of the day, and shade soils with mulch after planting.

Divide plants when they are not actively growing to reduce water loss and to allow roots to regenerate before top growth resumes.

IN THIS CHAPTER

Know Your Soil **24**

Soil Texture **26**

Planting and
Transplanting **33**

Water and
Xeriscaping **36**

Managing for Water
Conservation **38**

Ways to Water **40**

Fertilizers and
Nutrition **42**

Mulch **45**

Pest Management **48**

Use basic xeriscaping techniques in caring for your garden—working the soil, planting and transplanting, watering, fertilizing, mulching, managing pests—but don't take any one of them for granted as that can lead to being wasteful. One technique takes on a subtle change because another one is lacking.

Water is, perhaps, the most important element. It affects everything you do in the garden and every stage of plant growth. This chapter discusses soil, planting, fertilizers, weed and pest management, and irrigation, with emphasis on how each affects water use. The key to xeriscaping is to make the most of what you have without opting for less.

After reviewing the ideas in this chapter, you will be better equipped to approach each garden task from a perspective of xeriscaping. But also use your own experience. Once you have gardened for several seasons in an arid climate, you will have a good understanding of your site and a more intuitive sense for gardening in these dry conditions.

Know your soil

Soil is the growing medium for the plants in your garden. It is the upper layer of the earth's surface and consists of mineral and organic matter, air, and water. On your site, it may be native soil or it may be a "builder's special" with subsoil, concrete, wires, and other debris included. Whatever its composition, soil is your partner in cultivating plants. Your success with xeriscaping depends on how well you know your soil and how well you match plants to it. Plant performance is tied to soil type and condition.

The ideal garden soil for most plants, loam, is rare in the arid west. Loam is a medium-textured soil with a favorable combination of about 45 percent sand, silt, and clay and about 5 percent organic matter. This combination is suitable for growing many plants—those that grow in moist as well as arid climates and some that grow in wet soil. Loam holds moisture and nutrients yet allows water to drain so that air moves into the pores containing either air or water. The ideal soil moisture condition for plants is when the soil pores contain 25 percent air and 25 percent water. The amount of air in the soil at any one time depends on the amount

To quicken healing and regrowth after transplanting, use sharp tools when cutting plants.

Plants grown in hanging baskets need water more frequently than those grown in beds in the ground. Measure the amount of water a container-grown plant needs and water with care.

of water present in the soil pores. After a rain (or irrigation), there is more water and less air in the spaces; in dry periods, there is more air and less water. Good garden soil exists when water, air, plant roots, and organisms (such as fungi, bacteria, nematodes, and earthworms) are able to move freely through the soil's root zone.

Although loam is the ideal garden soil, it is not the norm. Soil forms under a variety of conditions (climate, bedrock, vegetation, and elevation). A gardener's success depends in large measure upon how the soil is managed.

Texture—the interaction of mineral particles of sand, silt, and clay—, organic matter, soil structure, and pH are all significant qualities of soil that affect gardening.

Harvest home-grown fruits and vegetables when they are young, tender and most flavorful.

Transplant when woody plants or herbaceous perennials are dormant and just before growth begins.

Soil Texture

Soil texture refers to the proportion of sand, silt, and clay in a given volume of soil and is identified on a scale from coarse to medium to fine.

COARSE SOILS include gravel, loose rock fragments, loamy sand, sandy loam, or sand. They are low in organic matter, low in fertility, low in chemical activity, and poor in water retention, especially in the top few inches. Water moves more quickly through coarse soil; the coarser the soil, the less it holds. In 1 foot of soil, sandy soil holds about ¼ inch of water, whereas sandy loam holds about ¾ inch. Plants that produce deep or coarse root systems, as well as those plants that fix nitrogen, are well-suited to these types of soil.

MEDIUM-TEXTURED SOILS (sandy loam, loam, sandy clay loam, and silty loam) retain air, water, and nutrients. Most plants grow well in these soils, although very drought tolerant plants can become gangly or rot with too much moisture.

FINE-TEXTURED SOILS have a high clay content. They include clay, silty clay, sandy clay, clay loam, and silty clay loam. Water moves more slowly through fine-textured soil. Silt to clay loam holds about 2½ to 3 inches of water in a foot of soil.

Soils with large amounts of clay have very different properties from those with more sand or silt. Clay soils are fertile, chemically active, retain water for long periods of time, and slow air flow through soil pores. Heavy clay soils are difficult to manage. They are sticky when wet and hard and lumpy when dry. Many types tend to shrink when dry and swell when wet. Because clay particles are minute, clay soil is prone to compaction and poor structure. Therefore you have to work with it when moisture levels are just right (not wet or dry). Xeric plants that normally grow in dry, coarse soil may rot in clay if soil water is not carefully managed. Water management is key with fine-textured soil.

Identify your soil texture by feeling it in your hands and rubbing a moistened soil sample between your fingers and thumb. Sandy soil feels gritty and not sticky. You can see and feel individual grains. When dry, it will not form

Layers in soil profiles vary in number, characteristics, thickness, and composition depending on soil type.

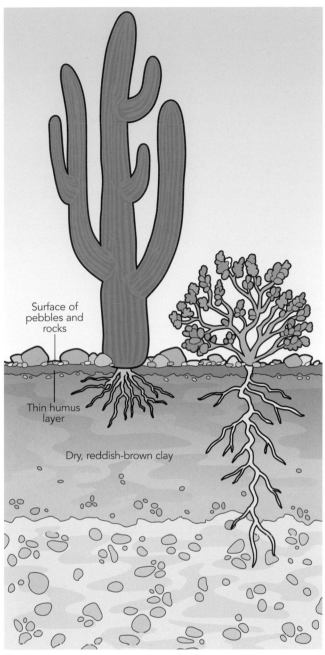

Many desert plants develop shallow surface roots to capture moisture from light rains; others send roots deep for water.

Grassland soils have a dark, thick layer rich in humus which supports good root growth.

a molded shape. If moist, it will mold into shape but crumbles with light pressure.

Loam is soft, crumbly, and manageable. It is slightly gritty to touch and slightly sticky when moist.

Silty soil feels smooth, silky, and somewhat plastic. You can mold it, but it will break apart if not handled carefully.

Clay is the most adhesive soil type. You can mold it into a long, thin, cigarlike shape. It will not break without some pressure.

Texture influences the workability of soil. Coarse, sandy to gritty soils are easier to work wet or dry because they break apart, whereas clay and silt hold together. A good

garden soil should be workable and hold together but break apart easily with slight pressure.

The texture of your soil is difficult to alter. Instead, learn how to work with the soil you have, perhaps gradually improving its structure by adding organic matter.

Soil Texture
continued

Soil structure

Workable soil is also influenced by soil structure, which is determined by how individual soil particles are bound together into aggregates. Some aggregates are easier to work with than others. Sand and clay have poor structure. Sand will not hold together under pressure when it is dry, and clay forms unworkable clods when dry. Poor soil structure can either slow or speed water drainage. A predominance of clay in soil slows drainage and sand speeds it up. Soils with good structure usually have a reasonable amount of organic matter. Organic matter improves fine-textured clay soils because it glues tiny particles into larger ones and creates bigger air spaces.

ORGANIC MATTER: Organic matter consists of debris from plants and small organisms in various stages of decay. The amount of organic matter varies from one soil type to another. In loam or in more humid, cooler environments, organic matter may make up 5 percent of soil by volume. However, it is much less in more arid and warmer environments. Desert soil usually has less than 1 percent organic matter because organic production is very slow under dry conditions. Unlike mineral particles that hold moisture on their surface, organic matter absorbs it. Increasing organic matter increases the soil's water-holding capacity if the material is decomposed. A workable garden soil should contain 3 to 5 percent organic material.

You can slowly improve soil texture over time with amounts of organic matter.

This is why healthy garden soil with a long history of cultivation is higher in organic matter and usually more productive.

Soil profile

Soils naturally develop into layers called horizons. The depth and the definition of each layer depend on the topography, region, and climate in which it develops. You can see a soil profile (sequence of layers from surface to bedrock) where land has been excavated for construction or where mountains have been sliced for roadways.

If conditions that form soil are favorable, there may be five to six horizons. Shortly after disturbance they may be absent. In a soil profile, the top layer is organic, consisting primarily of fresh and

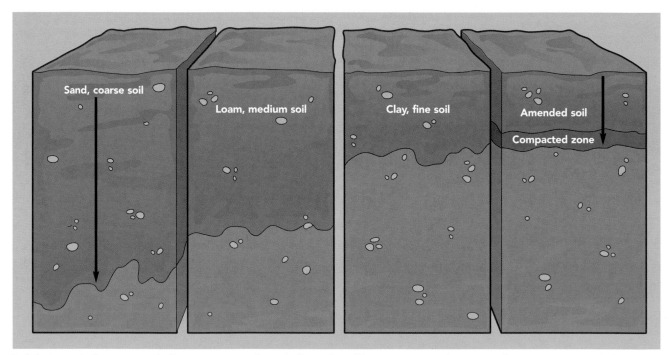

Soil drainage is the rate at which water moves through the soil profile. Here, an equal amount of water moves much deeper into sandy soil than clay soil. Water does not readily drain through compacted soil zones.

decomposing plant residue and small organisms. A deciduous forest usually has a thick organic layer because of continuous leaf litter. Deserts have a thin organic layer because most leaves are small and production is slow. The second layer is topsoil. This consists of mineral particles such as sand, silt, and clay and some decomposed organic matter. Plant roots are usually found in topsoil. Under the topsoil horizon is a layer where many of the nutrients from the two above layers have been leached. Together, the three layers make up the cultivated zone of gardens. Beyond the cultivated zone is subsoil. It is usually finer and firmer than the surface soil and has little if any organic matter. Developers often remove topsoil and leave subsoil. This can present problems for growing plants as subsoil can be difficult to work. Caliche is a naturally occurring subsoil desert hardpan (see hardpans, at right).

Beyond the subsoil is the parent material, consisting of decomposed rock or other materials, with characteristics similar to the subsoil and characteristics of the rock from which it came. Parent material influences soil texture, fertility, and pH. At the very base of the profile is bedrock.

Soil nearest the surface has most of the organic matter. Farther down from the top is less organic matter and more rock particles. In arid and semiarid climates, soils are often immature and poorly developed. Poorly developed soils also occur on steep hillsides and in sand hills. Even though these soils may be difficult for gardeners, in the natural world suitable plants have evolved and adapted to them. Growing plants from humid environments where organic matter is plentiful is a frustrating, time-consuming task in the arid west. You will be rewarded when you discover the types of plants that are better suited for their soil and environment.

Soil drainage

Providing good drainage is one of the most important things you can do for plants. The plant encyclopedia, beginning on page 84, indicates that most cultural recommendations stress "good drainage." Soil drainage is the rate at which an amount of water moves through the soil profile. Good drainage helps maintain air space for plant roots. The spaces fill with water in poorly drained soil. Without air, there is no oxygen. Plants need oxygen as well as water and nutrients for healthy growth.

To determine how well your soil drains, dig a 1×1-foot hole. Fill it with water and allow it to drain completely. Fill the drained hole again and measure how much the water level drops in hourly increments. If water drains 1 inch per hour, it is draining quickly. Most plants can grow under conditions where the water level drops between ¼-inch and 1 inch per hour. Pores are filled with air most of the time. Xeric plants from desert and semiarid environments are best grown in these sites.

If water drains less than ¼ inch per hour, soil is slow to drain. Plants that tolerate saturated soil do better here. If water remains more than 24 hours, there may be a hardpan or other problems. Correct any standing water as it is a potential breeding ground for mosquitoes.

HARDPANS: There are conditions that alter soil drainage such as hardpans, compaction, and insufficient rainfall. Hardpans occur when clay particles plug the pores and compact the soil. This can occur at the soil surface or in the subsoil. When pores become plugged, a hardpan develops, impeding drainage and root growth. There are different kinds of hardpans. Caliche (found in warm deserts) is a natural calcium carbonate cemented layer, several inches to 6 feet deep. A calcium carbonate layer may also produce a hardpan in short-grass prairie environments because of low precipitation, especially in summer. When water enters the soil, it moves through the various soil layers as far as it can according to the amount of rain and the soil's drainage. As it moves through the soil, it dissolves the calcium carbonate. If the amount of rainfall is low, the calcium carbonate may accumulate over time and form an impermeable layer. Hardpans contribute to poor aeration and salt accumulation at the soil surface.

Hardpans can develop for reasons that are not related to the climate. Heavy equipment or repeated foot traffic on heavy wet clay soils is a common cause of hardpan.

Soil Texture
continued

SALINE AND ALKALI SOIL:
Soils in arid regions often have high salt content. Salinity is an accumulation of soluble salts in areas of poor drainage where there isn't enough moisture to wash them through the soil. The problem is greater in fine-textured soils. Salts can also build up in a garden from repeated use of fertilizers and manure. High salts can prevent seed germination, retard plant growth, and burn foliage.

An alkali (sodic) soil is one with high amounts of sodium that negatively affects plant growth and soil structure. Both saline and alkali soil can be improved by providing good drainage and by washing or leaching the salts through the soil profile. Leaching will require water beyond the plant's root zone. Where this is not possible, there are plants that tolerate high salt levels.

Water may move up to the surface and carry soluble salts with it. It is common to find salts on the surface soil in arid areas. These are noticeable because of white, crusty particles in contrast with brown soil.

Soil pH and nutrition

Good nutrition is essential for healthy plants. The soil's ability to supply needed nutritional elements often depends on the soil pH and the plant's pH growing range.

Soil pH is measured on a scale from zero to 14. Below 7 to zero is acid; above 7 to 14 is alkaline; 7 is neutral.

Arid and semiarid environments often have alkaline soil. Humid areas are more acidic. Soil pH is important to plant growth because it affects the availability of nutrients. Most nutrients are available between pH 6 to 8.4. As the soil goes beyond this range, some nutrients become chemically tied up and

unavailable for plant use. For example, iron becomes unavailable when alkalinity is above pH 8.5. The amount of salt in the soil also tends to increase with alkaline soil.

Although both alkalinity and acidity can be modified, it is more practical, less frustrating, and often less expensive to select the appropriate plant for the site rather than changing the site for the plant. If the soil has a pH of 8.0 (alkaline), do not plant materials that require pH of 5.0. Appropriate plant selection means growing plants that will best tolerate the site and soil as they exist.

Soil amendment

Amendments are materials used to change pH, improve aeration and drainage of fine textured soil, or increase water and nutrient retention of coarse soil. Organic matter can be compost, sewage sludge, or well-rotted manure, among others. Organic matter should be a renewable resource, safe and not removed from a natural ecosystem. For semiarid and arid areas with saline soil, materials high in salts, such as sludge or manure, should be avoided because they compound the salt problem. Organic matter is considered ready to use as an amendment when it is mostly decomposed, odorless, and crumbly. The organic amendment may equal up to one third of the volume of the soil to be amended in order to make a significant change in garden soil. To change 1,000 square feet of soil add up to 3 inches of organic matter and work it into the existing top 6 inches of soil to make a 9-inch deep amended layer. You will need 333 cubic feet or 12⅓ cubic yards of material. You can also apply compost in holes dug into the garden or planting beds.

Once you have added the material, the soil is not automatically improved. Microorganisms, soil particles, and weathering interact. Through time soil gradually changes. Improving existing soil is a long-term project.

Another approach to amending soil is to grow a cover crop—a temporary, rapidly growing plant that can be incorporated into the soil after a few weeks or months. 'Elbon' ryegrass is an example. Sow seeds in late fall or early spring and then turn plants over into soil about two weeks before you are ready to plant. Cover crops are helpful in vegetable gardens and areas for lawns. They also protect the soil from erosion.

Soil preparation is effective for flowers, shrub, and vegetable gardens, but research shows that it is not necessary when planting large trees and shrubs. You must decide when it is practical or necessary to amend soil and what it will take to get the soil to a desirable condition.

Some researchers have found that plants grow better in unamended soil because roots tend to stay in amended soil if it is richer than the surrounding area. When plants grow in aerated, unamended soil, roots will develop beyond the planting hole into surrounding soil.

In some instances, xeric plants with succulent tissues or pubescent stems may rot when soil is amended with organic matter. Studies show that many plants establish and grow better if planted in soil similar to their native soil.

Mycorrhizae (inset) are special fungi that have a beneficial relationship with roots of many types of plants such as with this velvet mesquite (Prosopis velutina).

Soil Texture
continued

Plants adapted to dry regions are often susceptible to crown rot if planted too deep in soil that drains slowly. Especially in clay soils, plant high and on a firm base of soil. Make the planting hole as wide as practical.

To determine whether to amend, evaluate your soil, its texture, and its drainage; then decide what plants to grow based on the inherent plant/soil partnership. Amending soil is an ongoing process and is recommended in areas where high yields are expected (such as vegetable gardens) and where plants are removed annually (annual flower or vegetable gardens). Amendments are also desirable if you are preparing a bed of manageable size. Ultimately, providing good drainage is the most important thing you can do to improve the soil for plants. Soil that is compacted or has poor air movement may not need amending. The compacted or hardened soil may only need to be broken, tilled, or aerated. Hand spade the area for root penetration (this may need to be done several times) and break up any clods. You can slice or core holes into tight soil in some areas and allow plant debris or roots to fill in the holes.

Soils where amendments may be problematic are those with expansive clay (swells when wet and shrinks/cracks when dry) commonly found in semiarid grassland regions. These show problems if amended with organic matter and then irrigated. Swelling and shrinking may cause mud slides or may crack foundations. Working with expansive soil requires careful water management. Use plants native to these soils, such as those from a short-grass prairie, and manage water to prevent swings from wet to dry.

Careful management is a way to deal with difficult soil conditions. Growing plants with deep root systems combined with those that fix nitrogen and using mulch to reduce evaporation are practical ways of dealing with coarse soil, rather than adding materials to the soil to retain more moisture.

Inoculate soil with mycorrhizae, fungi that have mutually beneficial relations with living plant roots. New research suggests that mycorrhizae improve drought tolerance in plants either by improving phosphorus nutrition that enhances drought tolerance or by fungal strands that extend the roots' ability to harvest more soil moisture.

If you want professional help with your soil, you can send samples to professional laboratories or to the state cooperative extension service for analysis. Soil tests identify pH, texture, available nutrient elements, and salt problems. They also provide guidelines on fertilizer and soil amendments for specific plants. Soil-testing laboratories will provide complete fertilizer and soil amendment recommendations.

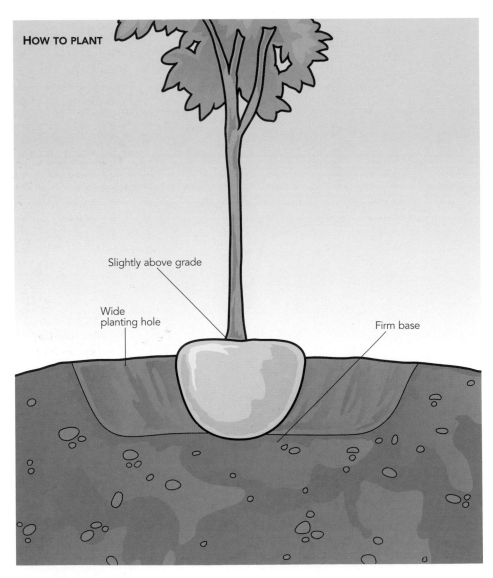

HOW TO PLANT

Slightly above grade

Wide planting hole

Firm base

Planting and Transplanting

Whether you are planting or transplanting, your goal is to move a plant into its new location with as little stress to the plant as possible. First select the right plant for the site. Once you have made this decision, use effective planting procedures—those that minimize root loss, prevent root damage, and reestablish the plant as quickly as possible.

MINIMIZE ROOT LOSS:
Be as gentle as possible when handling the plant to avoid breaking or injuring the roots. Whether plants are in a container, balled and burlapped, or transplanted from another site, removing them from existing soil loosens attached particles and causes some root injury. The less the root is damaged, the faster the plant will reestablish. However, if the roots are root-bound (coiled or wrapped around the soil ball), roughen and loosen the roots so they can grow into the surrounding soil. This is a common problem when plants stay too long in containers.

PREVENT ROOT DAMAGE:
Plant on a calm, cloudy, or cool part of the day. If it is too hot, wind and sun can dry exposed roots in seconds. Young seedlings also die quickly under these conditions. If you remove a plant from one site to another, keep as much soil around the roots as possible. If you plant from a container, wire basket, burlap, or other wrap, carefully place the plant in the hole and then loosen the material once the plant is situated. Cut the burlap, twine, fiber pots, or wire and gently remove it. If this is not possible, then remove all the material from the sides and leave the bottom material at the base of the plant. Yanking anything from under the plant destroys the root ball. In arid climates, these materials do not decompose. Always keep the soil ball covered until planting is completed.

Shade young or newly planted plants to minimize water loss until they become established.

Divide irises after their flowers fade when they are entering a dormant state.

When dividing plants such as sedum, use a sharp tool to make clean cuts and minimize damage to the plant's crown.

Planting and Transplanting
continued

Amend and shape soils according to the kinds of plants you intend to grow.

CHOOSE WHEN TO PLANT:
The best time for most plants is when they are dormant and before they are about to break bud. This often coincides with natural precipitation, usually in late winter to spring and late summer to early fall. Planting with the natural rhythm enables plants to become established with minimal supplemental irrigation if precipitation is sufficient. Summer heat and dryness are generally too difficult on transplants. Planting during this time consumes more water. In Mediterranean climates such as southern California, planting before the winter rains is recommended.

After the plants are established, watering becomes a personal choice or a function of availability. Although many xeric plants will grow without additional water, they may go dormant, may not flower, or may not be as attractive in the hot, dry periods. Supplemental watering can benefit the establishment of xeric plants.

Use similar techniques to plant and transplant herbaceous perennials. Move or divide them when they are still dormant. If they are not dormant, cut them back to minimize moisture loss. When they are lifted from the soil to be divided, dig the entire clump. Prepare the planting hole so that it is large enough to accommodate the roots plus an additional 4 to 5 inches wider. Loosen the roots before putting the plants in the hole. Keep the planting level the same as it was in the pot or in the soil where it was before being divided and transplanted. Space the plants twice as far apart as the expected height. Backfill with the soil until the hole is half full; then water. After the water is absorbed, fill the rest of the hole with soil and finish watering.

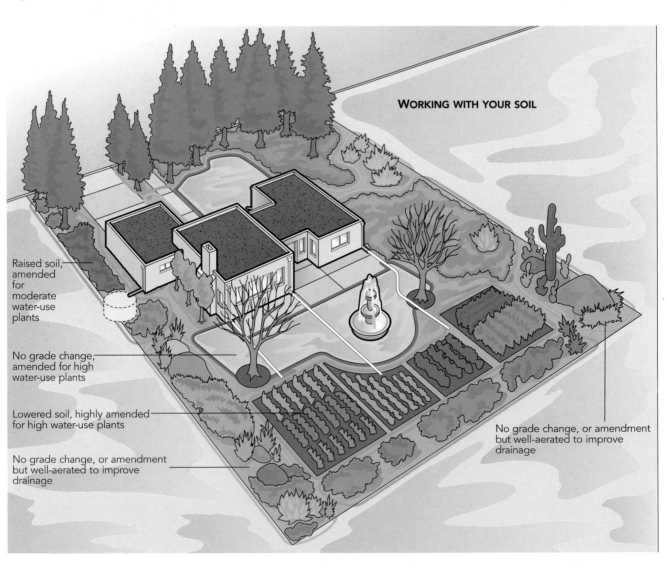

WORKING WITH YOUR SOIL

Raised soil, amended for moderate water-use plants

No grade change, amended for high water-use plants

Lowered soil, highly amended for high water-use plants

No grade change, or amendment but well-aerated to improve drainage

No grade change, or amendment but well-aerated to improve drainage

ESTABLISH THE PLANT:

Prepare the hole or bed prior to planting. Preparation will depend on what you are growing. If you are planting species native to an arid environment, aerate the soil by loosening it, breaking through any compacted layers, and removing or fracturing soil clods that may impede root growth. This may require an auger or pick axe to break through the hardpan until you reach a more porous horizon. If you can't break through a hardpan, such as caliche, create a drainage chimney or channel at the base of the planting hole. Do not add organic soil amendments. You may want to water the area several days prior to planting as this may make it easier to work with the soil. Fast-growing, high-yield plants such as fruits, vegetables, or annuals do best in a good garden loam. For these plants, add compost or other organic material.

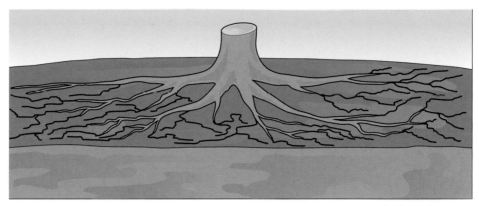

In fine-textured soil, dig the planting hole 2 to 3 times as wide (or more with unbreakable hardpan) as the root system and 1 to 2 inches shallower than the depth of the ball. Do not plant on loose ground because the plant will be below grade when the soil eventually settles. If the soil is coarse, plant at grade. Refill the hole with the native soil. Firm the soil around the plant, but do not stomp on it. With the extra soil, create a saucer around the plant or bed. This will prevent runoff and focus water on the root zone. Water thoroughly and mulch with the appropriate material (see page 45). Do not fertilize at the time of planting. Water the plant as needed until it is established. Depending on the plant, this can take six weeks for annuals and up to two years for trees or shrubs. Water when the soil is dry 4 to 6 inches below the surface for woody plants and 1 to 2 inches below the surface for herbaceous plants. Water thoroughly to moisten the planting hole or bed.

Thickened roots become thinner as they grow away from the center. The finer, smaller roots and root hairs absorb water and nutrients.

Roots develop differently in different soil types.

HOW SOIL AFFECTS ROOT DEVELOPMENT

Fibrous-rooted plant in loam (left), and clay (right) soils.

Tap-rooted plant (left), and fibrous-rooted plant (right) in sandy soil.

Water and Xeriscaping

Wilting leaves are a clear sign of water stress.

Xeriscaping evolved because of a need to conserve water in arid communities that have used too much supplemental water. Gardeners have grown a high percentage of plants native to, or developed in, humid environments. These plants require two to three times the amount of natural precipitation available to them in dry climates. Not only has irrigation allowed traditional types of gardens in arid environments, but it has permitted timely seed germination, soil preparation, planting, and harvesting. Many gardeners irrigate by habit rather than by need because watering has become so routine. Consequently, gardens and landscapes in the arid west are dependent on supplemental water, and irrigation has become as essential as any other gardening practice.

In recent years, drought and a growing population sharing the same resource have led to more frequent watering restrictions. You can no longer water when you want to but when your local water supply board determines it. In an extreme drought, you may not be able to water outdoors at all. Gardens planned for available natural resources will have a better chance of surviving than those dependent on supplemental watering. You can still enjoy gardening and create a beautiful and functional landscape. However, you have to be more aware of your soil and its capacity as a moisture reservoir. Learn about a chosen plant's growth, its needs, and its ability to hold onto water.

WATER AND PLANT GROWTH: Generally, plants from humid environments (more than 20 inches of rainfall per year) use water efficiently when it is available but are not able to conserve it, and thus are more sensitive to drought. By contrast, plants from arid environments (less than 20 inches of rainfall) with low relative humidity are not as efficient in water use and generally grow slowly, but are more effective in conserving water and less sensitive to drought. By matching plants with soil characteristics, you can create a water-conserving garden that prospers even in a drought.

Weeds choke out desirable grasses during extended drought.

ROOTS AND XERISCAPING:

Roots are the major conduits for providing water to plants. Roots branch out in a manner similar to above-ground plant structures. They are larger in diameter nearest the crown and gradually become thinner in diameter as they grow away from the center. The largest roots' major role is to transport water and nutrients; as these thickened roots narrow and branch, finer roots and root hairs emerge. These absorb water and nutrients. Trees and shrubs grow fine roots and hairs between the plant's drip line (outermost edge of upper branches) to halfway between the trunk or stem crown. If a tree has a 30-foot spread, the absorbing roots may be 15 to 45 feet or more away from the trunk. Herbaceous plants with fibrous roots (numerous roots that grow and spread close to the surface) have root hairs growing amid the intricate system. On taprooted or main-thickened roots of herbaceous perennials (like carrots), these hairs grow about one-third to halfway down between the crown almost to the root tips.

Additionally, most fine roots and root hairs grow in the top 6 to 18 inches of soil where there is moisture and oxygen. Roots do not grow where the soil is dry. If moisture is at the surface, that is where roots will be. If subsurface soil is moist and porous, roots will also grow there. Roots close to the surface are more vulnerable to drought. Whenever you water, apply enough to moisten the entire root zone. The more extensive and deeper the roots, the better the drought tolerance is. Note: Although some desert plant roots can grow down to a deep water table, this is more likely to occur in a natural environment where soil allows deep penetration. It is less common in urban environments where construction has disturbed the soil horizons and drainage patterns.

You can amend soil or improve drainage, but sometimes the soil is shallow because of bedrock or other conditions that cannot be corrected. Here, you can grow cacti and succulent plants with shallow or ephemeral roots. These plants have the ability either to draw on water reserves from their leaves or stems in times of stress or to develop rain roots when moisture is available. Many xeric plants are also sensitive to too much moisture and subject to crown or root rot when traditional gardening techniques (such as amending or mulching soil with organic material) are applied. If conditions exist where water drains too slowly and there is no way to improve it, you may try growing plants from wetland or riparian areas.

Like above-ground plant structures, roots branch out. Roots of some desert plants can reach great depths.

Many succulent plants, such as this aloe, are well suited to growing in thin, shallow soil, but they can show moisture stress when their root zones are limited, as in this container garden.

Managing for Water Conservation

In traditional gardening, you water for plant growth and for healthy plant maintenance. In xeriscaping, except for high-yield plants such as vegetables or fruits, you nurture plants until established to a desired state and then sustain them with minimal resources. You should water and fertilize with constraint.

To create a xeric garden, group plants together according to their water needs.

Plants respond differently to moisture at different stages of growth. Young plants are more sensitive to drought than older, more established plants. However, the demand for water depends more on the plant type, size, soil, sunlight, temperature, humidity, and wind than on the stage of plant growth. To reduce water demand, you can modify many of these factors.

Plants from more humid environments need more water in arid environments. Plants in sun transpire more than plants in shade. Plants in sandy soil need more frequent irrigation than those in clay soil.

All these factors can make watering confusing. The best way to know when to water is to watch for signs of water stress, such as wilt in plants

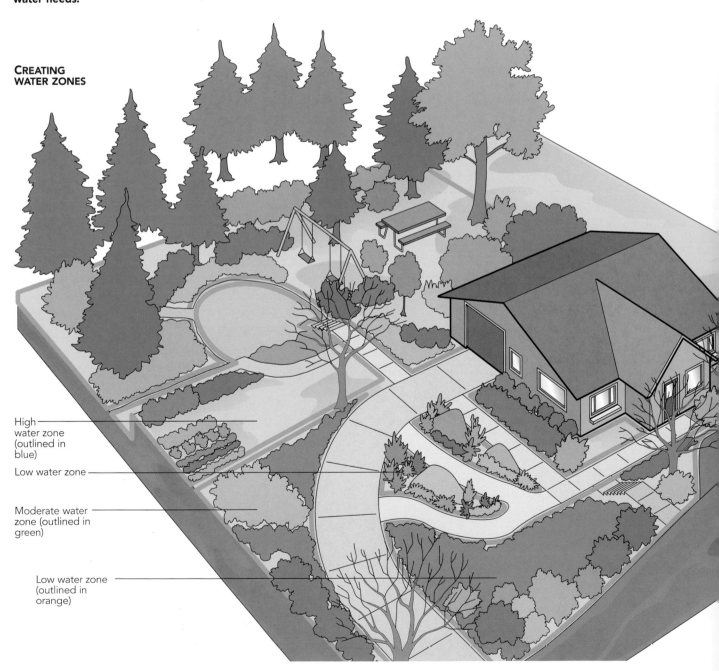

CREATING WATER ZONES

High water zone (outlined in blue)

Low water zone

Moderate water zone (outlined in green)

Low water zone (outlined in orange)

with larger leaves (sentinel plants for example). Wilt first appears when the surface soil becomes dry. On smaller, coarse, thick, or succulent leaves, look for signs of shrinkage, yellowing, or discoloration, and leaf drop.

Let your plants tell you when they need water. Soft plants, such as lawn grass, annuals, and perennials, wilt shortly after soil moisture is depleted so are better indicators than other plants that respond more slowly.

PROTECTING SOIL MOISTURE: Make the most of what you have by protecting the soil surface. Water loss from soil is caused by roots extracting the water, as a result of plant

transpiration, and evaporation from the surface. Evaporation seldom occurs below 6 inches. Even deep sand is moist beyond the surface. Keep moisture in the soil by minimizing cultivation, as it promotes evaporation, and by maintaining a soil cover either with plants, a mulch, or dried plant residue. If soil is exposed, or if vegetation is too close to the surface, the soil has a greater chance of becoming compacted. If this occurs, there is little to break the force of water from irrigation or rainfall, and much will simply run off. A good ground cover or mulch increases water absorption and also decreases soil temperature and evaporation. Poor soil cover increases drought conditions even if moisture is available.

WATERING ZONES: In a well-planned xeric garden, plants are placed together not only by aesthetic and functional appeal but also by their water and cultural needs. This allows you to water and care for them with minimal water waste because they all need the same treatment. These groupings are called water zones, or hydrozones. Water zones are typically divided into low, medium, and high water requirements. Low water zone plants (once established) survive mostly on natural precipitation and require the least amount of watering. Moderate water zone plants may need occasional watering, especially during dry periods. Regular or higher water zones consist of plants that require water on a fairly regular basis throughout the growing season. These plants should be kept to a minimum and planted in areas

where you can harvest rainwater from eaves, or in areas adjacent to other high water zones where you can take advantage of the runoff. Areas adjacent to irrigated lawn, or the base of a slope where plants collect runoff, are two examples.

By focusing on water zones, you can efficiently control the amount, time, and placement of water. Your garden may have one or more zones depending on your plant selection, site, and soil. A low water zone might consist of desert plants, such as acacia, cacti, and yucca planted in full sun in gravelly soil. A moderate water zone might consist of prairie plants, dryland perennials, or ornamental grasses in full sun in sandy loam. A high water zone may be a garden clay loam with vegetable or fruit trees or plants from more humid environments. The amount of water applied to any one zone will be the difference between natural precipitation and the plant use. A high water use zone, such as a vegetable garden, uses about 6 inches of water per month or 24 inches for four months. If your environment receives 12 inches during that same time period, you will need to apply 12 more inches.

In low to moderate water zones, you can apply water when plants show signs of water stress, such as wilting leaves and stems or premature foliage drop. In high water zones, fluctuation from moist to dry can be detrimental at certain stages of plant growth such as flower or fruit set. Under these conditions, the soil should be kept evenly moist.

Ways to Water

Soaking areas of the original root ball of new plants is vital the first few months after planting.

You usually water by hand only when plants need it.

There are many ways to water. Consider first how plants are arranged. Mass plantings are likely to be easier to water with broadcast sprinklers, while individual plants or small groupings may be easier to water with basin, furrows, or bubbler techniques. Keep in mind that trees and shrubs have roots that extend horizontally to or even beyond their outer branches. To conserve water and to use it efficiently, apply the water where the fine roots and root hairs are.

You can water by hand and save on an irrigation system. This works well if your garden is fairly independent of supplemental water, although dragging hoses across the yard can sometimes damage plants and is often clumsy, except when hose bibbs are in the right locations. However, you are more likely to water plants only when they need it and not out of habit because hand watering is time consuming.

To conserve water, you need to know the depth from which soil water is being extracted. If there are no active roots in the soil, moisture removal is slow. When you apply water, stop before the entire root zone is wet and allow the water to move at its own pace. By the next day, the water should have moved to fill the root zone. If not, you may have to add more water. As a guide, lawn roots are 6 inches deep, and roots of shrubs and perennials in prepared soil are 12 inches deep.

To simplify hand watering, create a ring of soil around individual trees or shrubs or a basin around the entire planting bed. When you water, fill the basin with the amount of water needed to moisten the entire root zone. If you are planting in rows, create furrows between where water can flow and be absorbed into the soil. This type of watering works well in coarse soil. A perforated hose placed along the row also distributes water evenly.

Many gardeners prefer irrigation systems. There are various types available for home gardens. An irrigation system can be automated, completely manual, or it can be somewhere between. There are two types of systems: high- and low-volume irrigation.

Overhead sprinklers are high-pressure systems that apply water in fanlike sprays over the surface. Most of the components are underground with only the spray heads visible. They are by far the most common and work where vegetation is fairly uniform, such as in lawns or low ground covers with fibrous root systems and in coarse soils where intake is high. Water waste from evaporation, drift, and runoff is one disadvantage; another is automatic systems that operate regardless of need. Unless the planting beds are designed to match the spray heads, these overhead sprinklers are also not selective in what they water.

Microirrigation is a low-pressure and low-volume system that distributes water at a very slow rate. Water is applied in droplets (drip emitters), by barely visible sprays (microspray systems), or by bubblers. Bubblers are similar to spray heads but deliver a larger quantity of

Sprinklers that spray water high into the air lose water to wind and evaporation before it even reaches the soil.

Bubblers look like familiar spray heads but only soak plants that are close by.

water to small areas less than 5 feet in circumference. Because water is applied at the soil level, less is lost to evaporation and runoff. In a well-planned system, the root zone stays moist, but the surface remains dry. Microirrigation components are usually above ground on the surface or hidden under mulch. Low-pressure systems are best in fine-textured soil, in small yards; in vegetable, shrub, and flower beds; in container gardens and in hanging baskets.

Subsurface irrigation is similar to drip except that it waters from underground. Water moves and drains through connected perforated pipes beneath the soil surface. It provides water to roots laterally with little waste beyond the root zone. This type of system is gaining popularity with golf courses because of increased need for water conservation.

Whatever your system, always adjust your watering practices for the season, the plants, and the weather. The easiest and least expensive way is to become very familiar with your garden and plants. You can also try various sensors designed to monitor water systems. Sensors are devices that help the system respond to environmental conditions. Some interrupt irrigation if it rains or if humidity indicates rain is imminent. Others detect wind speed and suspend irrigation when winds are too strong. Soil moisture sensors control irrigation by measuring moisture levels in the soil. No matter what sensors you use, you must install and use them correctly to avoid potential water waste.

Microirrigation systems that apply water directly to the soil are efficient and highly effective.

Fertilizers and Nutrition

Fertilizers are essential plant nutrients provided to improve plant health and growth. Generally, they are applied with water or applied to the soil, although some can be sprayed directly on the foliage. In a natural environment, nutrients remain in the soil through plant death, decomposition, and natural recycling. In many traditional gardens, nutrients are often removed through cleanup practices and then replaced with soil amendments or commercial fertilizers. In xeriscape gardens, you should allow plant materials and nutrients to be returned to the soil. Commercial fertilizers are not often used because they encourage growth and greater water needs. However, there are times when fertilizers are needed, such as when you grow high-yield plants and when plant debris is removed without allowing it to recycle.

The same organic matter and compost that improves soil texture and structure also provides essential plant nutrients. You can improve soil nutrition by adding compost or other organic amendments on a seasonal basis. This approach is in

Garden debris and kitchen waste are important compost ingredients.

FERTILIZERS AND ESSENTIAL PLANT NUTRIENTS

The nutrients plants need are in the soil, air, and fertilizers. This latter category is the one gardeners control most. Fertilizers are organic or inorganic. Organic ones are from living organisms such as compost and manure. Inorganic fertilizers are manufactured. Never apply more than is recommended on the label.

keeping with xeriscaping and making the most of what you have. Composting may not be sufficient for a variety of reasons, depending on what you are growing. In this case you may need to add nutrients through a commercial fertilizer.

Every package of fertilizer states its contents. The percentage of the three major nutrients—nitrogen, phosphorus, and potassium—appears on the front of the package. These elements are always listed in that order. The absence of any is indicated by a zero. Other nutrients are listed elsewhere on the package. Western soils are usually low in nitrogen primarily because they are also low in organic matter. Nitrogen is rapidly used by plants or it is easily leached through the soil profile. Phosphorus is sometimes

deficient in clay soil. It does not move in the soil nor is it leached. Iron is not available in soil with high pH. Overall it is easier to grow plants that are adapted to the particulars of the soil and the site than to change the soil chemistry.

Fertilizers are best applied right before new growth when the plant will use it. For appropriate fertilizer recommendations for your soil and plants, contact your cooperative extension agent.

Composting

Xeriscaping is an environmentally friendly approach to gardening with minimal negative impact. Composting is environmentally friendly because it recycles and converts yard and kitchen waste into a renewable resource for your garden while it also saves space in landfills. In the natural world, recycling organic materials is easily seen in a forest where fallen leaves decompose and nutrients are returned to the soil for new plant growth. Bacteria, fungi, worms, and other organisms decompose organic material into their basic elements. The final product is a dark, friable compost that you can use in a garden as a soil amendment, potting mix, mulch, or top dressing.

BASICS OF COMPOSTING:

Composting depends on microorganisms digesting organic materials. Garden composting means providing these organisms with environmental conditions that meet their needs. These include optimum air, moisture, and nutrition.

■ **Aerobic microorganisms** that do most of the composting are aerobic. They require oxygen to

Build a compost pile by alternating a layer of high-nitrogen green materials with a layer of high-carbon brown materials.

do their work; otherwise, anaerobic organisms take over, slow down the process, and create an unpleasant odor. It is important to create abundant air space in the compost by providing various sizes of waste. Wet leaves by themselves may mat and

eliminate air. Mix them with fruit scraps, straw, or small twigs to keep the material porous. In addition, you can keep the compost aerated by stirring or turning it over regularly. Keeping the compost moist and aerated speeds the process.

Finished compost from a well-decayed pile goes into a wheelbarrow for use throughout the garden.

Fertilizers and nutrition
continued

Compost improves soil and adds nutrients. Cultivate it in, or leave it on top as a mulch.

■ **Soil microorganisms** also need moisture—not too wet to eliminate air and not too dry to impede growth—a texture something like a squeezed wet sponge. Green plant debris and fruit and vegetable scraps have sufficient moisture. However, you may have to periodically moisten the pile in arid areas.

■ **Food microorganisms** need brown plants high in carbon and green plants high in nitrogen because their activity is affected by a carbon nitrogen (C/N) ratio of organic material. Browns include dry and dead plant debris such as old leaves, twigs, and straw.

Greens include fresh weeds, grass clippings, fruit and vegetable scraps, tea bags, and coffee grounds, among others. Use an even mix of both.

PARTICULARS OF COMPOSTING: Composting occurs at 50° F or above. The process may go dormant in winter but resumes when the weather is warm. Composts are not always hot. The temperatures depend on how large the pile is. The larger the pile, the more insulation and the higher the temperature. The smaller the pile, the less insulation and the lower the temperature in cold weather.

Compost is finished when it becomes a dark, friable, earthy soil-like material. Most plant parts are unrecognizable, although sometimes you can identify plant fragments. A finished compost may be subjective. If you can recognize some leaves, you can still work the compost into the soil where final decomposition will occur. A fully composted pile will have fine nonrecognizable particles.

Materials to avoid in compost are meat scraps, fats, dairy products, bones, chemically treated wood products, diseased plants, pet or human wastes, and noxious weeds or weedy plant seeds.

OPTIONS FOR COMPOSTING: You can compost below the soil surface in trenches or holes dug 8 inches deep. Then plant above the compost. You can build a compost pile on the ground or create one with some type of container. Generally containers are either bins or drum tumblers. The type of composter you choose should be one that best suits your needs and capabilities.

Shredded leaves make an excellent mulch, and add organic matter to the soil as they decompose.

Mulch

Mulching is used in traditional gardens to modify a plant's growing environment. It also plays an important role in xeriscaping because it helps retain soil moisture, reduces weed competition, prevents soil crusting, protects soil structure, and protects bare soil from erosion. Mulch can also be aesthetic and unify planted areas. Mulch is available in different types, each with its own characteristics. You can buy in bags or in bulk. You can also make your own by recycling plant litter.

MULCH TYPES ARE DIVIDED INTO TWO GROUPS organic and nonorganic. Organic mulch comes from plant byproducts, such as wood and bark chips, sawdust and shavings, peanut shells, straw, grass clippings, leaf mold, leaf litter, pine needles, and compost. Organic mulch will decompose over time and become part of the soil. This is a great advantage because its decomposition adds organic matter to the soil. It also means that organic mulch needs replenishing. How quickly it decomposes and needs replacing depends on size of the material, the composition, and weathering.

All mulches have different characteristics that make them appropriate in various situations. Some have temporary uses while others have more permanent uses. Use temporary mulches seasonally to retain moisture and inhibit weed growth in flower and vegetable gardens. Or use permanent mulches for paths and around trees and shrubs. Permanent mulches are often a nice finishing touch to a garden.

Select a mulch that will benefit your environment and your garden style. Many mulches are byproducts of natural resources. If these resources are part of your environment, they will be less costly. Mulch is most attractive when it is used in harmony with the natural habitat of the plantings. There may be situations where no mulch is needed or ground cover may be a better choice.

ORGANIC MULCH can be decorative and/or functional. Most decorative mulch is from tree bark, either shredded, in chips, or in chunks. These mulches buffer soil from compaction, do not blow away, are attractive, and decompose slowly. Bark mulches are best used in forest gardens. Bark chunks, sometimes called nuggets, are decorative, can be very effective in weed management, but they move easily. They are best used in formal planting beds. Another tree product is wood mulch. This varies depending on the source. Wood mulch is created by pruning and chipping debris from a variety of trees (usually hardwoods) and shrubs. It has some of the same qualities of bark mulch but is not as uniform, consistent, or decorative as bark mulch. Sometimes wood mulch is given away by municipalities. Make sure that your source has used only disease-free trees before using this mulch.

Dried leaves also make a decorative and functional mulch. Pine needles are attractive, decompose slowly, and are easy to work. They work well in naturalized open woodland or prairie gardens, and are available commercially or where municipalities remove them from public land. Leaves from broadleaf evergreen or deciduous trees, such as oak, ash, or hackberry, are a good mulch if the leaves have been shredded with a composting mower or chipper. They work well under chaparral and shrubland plantings.

Chipped wood

Bark nuggets

Pine needles

Pea gravel and small, round river stone

Red lava rock

Mulch
continued

Other mulches include compost, leaf mold, grass clippings, and straw. These are often temporary and can be incorporated into the soil as an amendment at the end of the season. Sawdust mulch is best used on a garden path and not with vegetation because its decomposition removes nutrients from the soil.

APPLYING ORGANIC MULCH:
For very fine materials such as compost, mulch should be 1 to 2 inches deep. For coarse, fluffy material such as shredded bark, it should be 3 to 4 inches thick. For maximum benefit, mulch deeply enough to prevent weed seedlings from growing above the mulch and thick enough to conserve moisture in the top 6 to 8 inches of the soil surface.

Mulch should be several inches away from any woody trunk to prevent a hiding place for small rodents and to prevent rot. Do not apply organic mulch to succulent or dryland herbaceous plants because it creates a moist environment for microorganisms that cause stems, roots, or crowns to rot.

NONORGANIC MULCH:
Nonorganic mulches are derived from rocks, rubber, plastic, and other synthetic or man-made products.

Unlike organic mulch, they cannot be easily incorporated into the soil, do not improve the soil, are more permanent, and may raise ambient air temperatures. Rock mulch also tends to work free of planting beds and scatter onto paths and lawns.

Stone mulch and appropriate dryland plants combine here to make an attractive, low water use garden.

■ **Rock** byproducts include a variety of stone and gravel sizes. Crushed stone, gravel, and volcanic rock are available in a variety of textures, colors, and materials. Crushed stone, decomposed granite, small gravel, and coarse sand work best in xeric and rock gardens, or around desert shrubs and other xeric plants. With various rock sizes you can create a desert pavement surface for a desert garden. Use small pebbles, crushed stone, or decomposed granite as the base and scatter two or three sizes of flat sand or limestone pieces. Stone mulches go well with plants that thrive in dry soil. They should be applied 1 to 2 inches thick.

A layer of shredded bark around a newly planted tree slows evaporation of water from soil and improves tree growth.

■ **Plastics** as a mulch have been widely used but are not recommended with permanent plantings. They interfere with air exchange between the atmosphere and the soil. They also inhibit the water flow for plants that depend on natural precipitation. Plastic mulch is best used in vegetable gardens where irrigation systems are underneath them.

■ **Fabric mulches** made from polypropylene or polyester allow water and fertilizer to enter the soil. Generally the fabric has to be covered with another mulch to improve its appearance and keep it in place. Before laying it down, free the surface of weeds, especially pernicious weeds. Then add a thick layer of dressing of a more decorative mulch to prevent weed growth through the fabric. Make sure the aesthetic mulch does not create a slippery surface.

Mulch of stones around a rhododendron reflect enough heat to burn the leaves. This is an inappropriate mulch for the plant.

Pest Management

Xeriscaping is not just about saving water; it is also about protecting resources and the environment by developing a sustainable, healthy garden. A healthy garden is one where plants thrive with minimal pest management because healthy plants generally deal with problems on their own. All gardens may still have uninvited guests at some time. It is when these pests get out of control that they become a problem. Weeds, insects, disease, and sometimes small animals are considered pests when they interfere with, damage, mar, or decrease the vigor of a plant or garden. In a natural environment, damage is rarely noticed unless numerous plants show visible symptoms such as dead branches from a disease or insect outbreak. In a garden, you see injury more quickly even when it may affect only one plant.

The basic prescription for a healthy garden is to allow it to work with nature and

Pretty in pink bloom, tamarisk *(Tamarix parviflora),* is a noxious weed in many western states.

Lady bugs are natural predators that feed on undesirable garden insects such as aphids.

establish a balance. However, you should monitor the garden regularly so potential pests are discovered early. If there is a problem, you need to decide at what level its damage is tolerable. Aphids on a shade tree may be more tolerable than aphids on Brussels sprouts. Mildew on zinnias at the end of the season is more tolerable than in summer during their peak flowering. The question is whether the pest will damage the plants' overall vigor, use, or aesthetics.

INSECTS: There are ways to plant your garden so that it has a better chance of staying healthy and warding off problem insects. First, create plant diversity to limit opportunities of spreading the problem. A diverse garden can also provide food and shelter for natural predators such as ladybugs, praying mantises, and spiders— all of which feed on many undesirable insects. Second, use pesticides only when necessary. Many insecticides harm beneficial insects as well as the pests. If a pesticide is

necessary, apply it only to the problem. Third, plant the right plant in the right spot to advance plant health. Many healthy plants produce their own ways of controlling undesirable insects. Shrubby cinquefoil (a high-elevation plant) is often grown in hot, sunny sites at low elevations and becomes more susceptible to spider mite in this environment. Piñon pine grown in irrigated lawns becomes highly susceptible to pitch borer.

DISEASE: There are two categories of plant disease— infectious diseases caused by bacteria, viruses, or fungi; and noninfectious diseases caused by environmental or cultural conditions, like air pollution, water stress, or high salts. An infectious disease needs a host plant (lilac, for example), a pest (such as a fungus), and an environmental condition (high relative humidity) for symptoms (powdery mildew) to develop. Many diseases can be avoided if one of the three elements is eliminated. For example, grow plants resistant to mildew. This eliminates the host. Use drip irrigation instead of overhead spray. This reduces humidity around the foliage. You can also prevent disease by alternating or rotating plant species in vegetable and flower gardens. This can prevent disease buildup. Any time a disease occurs, discard the plant debris. Do not compost it.

Many problems that appear to be an infectious disease are often caused by cultural conditions. Fluctuations in temperature, pollution, or poor drainage may produce symptoms similar to diseases caused by microorganisms. Blackened twigs are a symptom both of bacterial fire blight and of frost damage. Many noninfectious diseases can be managed by selecting the proper plants, planting disease resistant varieties, and providing appropriate growing conditions.

WEEDS: A weed is more than a plant out of place. It is a plant that is aggressive, growing in areas without natural controls, is highly efficient in seed or vegetative reproduction, and has a high potential of becoming invasive. Weeds are plants that take advantage of a constantly changing environment. Over the last 15 years, numerous plants have become serious threats to natural systems and agriculture because of disturbance. Many have been declared as noxious. A noxious weed is legally prohibited from federal, county, and state lands. Noxious weeds are generally problems because they are in a foreign environment without their natural controls. Some of these weeds have been

inadvertently introduced as a contaminant with seeds, mulch, or manure; others have hitchhiked on animal fur, vehicles, and nursery-grown plants. In their desire to try new plants gardeners unknowingly bring them in from other parts of the country or world. Purple loosestrife, pampas grass, Russian olive, and tamarisk are noxious weeds in the arid west. Before introducing a new plant, check your county and state's noxious weed list. Even if they are not on the list, be aware of new plants and potential problems. Watch them carefully. See how quickly they establish, reseed, and spread.

Weed management for the gardener involves various methods. The first is prevention. When planting lawn, buy certified seeds. Watch for weeds in manure, containers, and field-grown stock. Use safe soil amendments such as homemade compost that has been made without weed seeds and cover crops. Avoid disturbing or exposing the soil as this invites invasive plants. Mulch the soil to prevent weed seedlings from growing. Remove weeds when they are small because they compete with your garden plants for water and nutrients.

There are times when you have to choose between using chemical herbicides or losing your plants. Chemicals used to be the first line of defense in managing pests, but they can damage desired plants as well as the weeds. Select the safest herbicide that will do the job. Read the label and follow directions with vigilance.

Pampas grass (Cortaderia selloana) can overwhelm native plants in natural environments.

WHAT IS IPM?

Integrated Pest Management (IPM) orchestrates various techniques to encourage a healthy, balanced system with minimal use of pesticide.

CULTURAL CONTROLS
- Choose the right plant for the site.
- Grow resistant varieties.
- Rotate and/or mix plants in vegetable gardens.
- Clean up debris where insects/disease overwinter.
- Plant at the right time.

PHYSICAL CONTROLS
- Hand pick or weed.
- Mow for weeds.
- Create barriers for insects.
- Trap for undesirable insects.

BIOLOGICAL CONTROLS
- Create environments for beneficial insects.
- Use natural predators and parasites.

SAFE PESTICIDE CONTROLS
- Use the least toxic chemical control available that is effective for the pest.
- Try vinegar for weeds and alcohol for insects.
- Use insecticidal soaps.

How to Xeriscape

IN THIS CHAPTER

Shaping a Xeriscape
Garden **51**

Conserving
Resources **55**

Creating Dry
Gardens **60**

Silver and Blue
Gardens **61**

Ornamental Grass
Gardens **64**

Sculpture Gardens **68**

Prairie Gardens **70**

Traditional Gardens
Xeric Style **76**

Victorian Gardens **82**

Gardens should provide pleasure. They become dissatisfying only when organized against the elements of the site and the environment. If a garden in an arid environment is organized with plants from humid areas, it automatically increases the need for resources, doubles or triples the maintenance, and often produces plants of inferior quality. Conservation of resources is the foundation of xeriscape. The fundamental building block of a garden is reduction of waste by reusing and recycling materials. This chapter presents various approaches to developing gardens with this philosophy. Great gardens do not have to be arduous or wasteful.

ELEMENTS OF A XERIC GARDEN

Driveway slopes towards lawn carrying runoff to turf

Runoff from roof is directed to landscape areas or collected in a cistern for use in irrigated zones

Runoff from roof is directed through downspouts, then through pipes to high-water-use areas such as the vegetable garden and home orchard

Bermed soil prevents runoff and keeps water in yard

Shaping a Xeriscape Garden

There are several elements involved in shaping an efficient xeriscape garden.

PLAN THE GARDEN: Many gardeners are interested in growing untried plants and often buy them before they know where to grow them. This often means putting the plant in the wrong location or squeezing it in where there is some open space. It is much more efficient and effective to plan the garden first and then select the plants that suit the plan and the growing conditions. You will reap rewards much earlier.

GROW PLANTS THAT MAKE SENSE IN THE ENVIRONMENT: This book stresses that choosing the right plant for the right spot is one of the most significant decisions you make in a xeriscape. How well the plant suits the site is strongly tied to the plant's ability to grow, tolerate stress, and fight disease. Choose plants best adapted to your environment. Native (indigenous) species and adapted plants usually offer a genetic background to survive your general environmental and climate conditions. There are also many introduced cultivated species that are better suited to the modified and created conditions found in areas such as altered urban and suburban locations.

If you do select a potentially consumptive plant, find the microclimate that best suits its needs or set aside a testing area to see what it actually takes to be successful. If the right location doesn't exist, select a different plant. There are many plants that may be more suitable. New species and cultivars appropriate to western gardens are becoming available all the time. You can find out what is available through garden catalogs, horticulture schools, and the plant introduction programs at botanic gardens and arboreta. This is an exciting time for western gardeners because many are becoming trendsetters in xeric gardening, not only by introducing new plants but experimenting with unconventional designs and plant combinations.

Trees and shrubs create wind barriers and shade more sensitive plantings

Native and adapted dryland plants grow in arid zones that receive little irrigation

Contoured terrain retains water on site

Shaping a Xeriscape Garden
continued

Select plants with xeric qualities, such as blue gramagrass, a warm-season western native.

EVALUATE THE SITE: Gardens are international. Lawn grasses originated in temperate Europe, many annuals and vegetables came from subtropical and tropical America, numerous herbs were introduced from the Mediterranean. In a garden you unite and encourage these plants from very different backgrounds to grow on the same property under the same environmental conditions. Before placing any plant in the ground, evaluate the elements (weather, sun and shade patterns, and soil) and how they affect the plant's ability to grow as you want. Anticipate what resources it will take to grow and picture how the plant will acclimatize through each season. Your chances of success are higher if you do this reality check.

SELECT PLANTS WITH XERIC QUALITIES: Three general water-use qualities affecting plant selection involve the plant's innate growing season, its root system, and its ability to spread. Many grasses, vegetables, and flowering plants are classified as cool- or warm-season species. Cool-season plants do most of their growing in spring and fall when soil temperatures (50° to 65° F) and air temperatures (60° to 75° F) are cooler. They flower from late spring to early summer. Warm-season plants are most active with soil temperatures from 70° to 90° F and air temperatures around 80° to 95° F. These flower from midsummer through fall. During summer months in arid environments, it takes more water to maintain cool-season plants than warm-season ones.

Plants in general become more drought tolerant once they are established. This is in part because root systems and storage structures (such as bulbs) develop and spread to access a broader range of available water and nutrients. Use this to your advantage

Palo verde trees are taprooted and good companions to more shallow-rooted plants such as pink Mexican evening primrose.

in a xeric garden. Locate taprooted species (since they are difficult to move) and bulbs first, then plant fibrous-rooted species around or above them. Combine plants based on their root systems to create interesting combinations above ground by using different levels of soil moisture and nutrients below ground.

The spreading quality of a plant also affects its use of water. Plants that spread, sprawl, or branch out quickly use more resources. Plants that grow more slowly use resources more slowly.

Use cool-season, spreading and thirsty Kentucky bluegrass sparingly in the arid west.

Erysimum 'Bowles Mauve' needs little water in regions with cool summers and mild winters.

A world of plants— columbine, delphinium, iris, salvia, wormwood— grow here in the same garden, receiving the same treatment.

Shaping a Xeriscape Garden
continued

The lavender, sage, and yarrow in this diverse planting thrive with little water.

A variety of well-adapted, high water use plants combine to produce a hardy garden, but should be limited in size.

WHEN SELECTING PLANTS, CREATE DIVERSITY: Using too many of the same species in your garden can present a problem later on. The same plant species in large numbers develop as a unit within the same time frame, using the same resources. When resources are not available, all of these plants are affected. If you plan for a variety of species with different stages of growth, plants do not compete for the same resources at the same time. And if a disease breaks out, only one species may be affected, but the rest of the garden survives. Diversity also helps in planning a garden to be interesting all four seasons.

LIMIT THIRSTY PLANTS: Keep high-moisture plants to a minimum. Lately, there has been a rebellion against lawns, blaming them for high water use. In truth, the problem is that many yards are planted with turfgrass that is totally dependent on irrigation. Of the thousands of grass blades that make up a lawn, each has to be perfect—no disease, no insects, and no weeds. The resources and energy used to meet these standards are excessive.

CONSIDER YOUR LAWN IN THE HOME GARDEN: Lawns cool the atmosphere, unify the landscape, allow heavy foot traffic, provide a recreational surface, and regrow within a season when damaged. Lawns are not the problem; it is the way you plant, use, and care for a lawn that affects the environment.

Instead of lawn, low groundcovers spread among boulders in a natural manner.

Conserving Resources

Native buffalograss makes an attractive and well-adapted lawn in some areas of the west.

REDUCE THE SIZE OF THE LAWN: Grow lawn only where you need it—in recreational and play areas. Avoid using lawn on steep slopes, in shady areas, in narrow spaces, or in other areas that are difficult to water and mow. Where appropriate, use groundcovers in lieu of a lawn. Generally groundcovers require less care and water while offering different textures and interest to your property. They should be tall enough to inhibit weeds, dense enough to shade the soil and minimize evaporation, and attractive throughout most of the year. Plants that qualify as groundcovers are herbaceous or woody, low-growing species that spread or sprawl and cover the ground within two to three seasons. They may spread by underground stems such as creeping hollygrape *(Mahonia repens)*, above-ground stems such as barren strawberry *(Waldsteinia ternata)*, or sprawl from above ground with long reaching branches such as creeping junipers *(Juniperus horizontalis)*. Many perennials and shrubs, when used in large groups, can perform as groundcovers.

ALTER PRACTICES: Many gardeners spend enormous time, money, and resources keeping the lawn green and weed free. Reconsider having a perfect lawn. Some plants, such as clover, were once thought of as weedy but are actually beneficial. Clover adds nitrogen to the soil, minimizes the need to fertilize, and attracts bees—important pollinators for fruit and vegetable production. (If bee stings are a concern, of course, eliminate the clover from your lawn.)

MOW THE LAWN HIGHER: High mowing reduces crabgrass and other weeds as well as soil evaporation. Kentucky bluegrass should be mowed to 2½ inches, perennial rye 2½ inches, and tall fescue 4 inches.

ALLOW CLIPPINGS TO REMAIN ON THE LAWN: Grass clippings left on the lawn reduce the need to fertilize.

GROW THE RIGHT GRASS FOR YOUR ENVIRONMENT: Instead of growing a cool-season lawn, consider a warm-season one. A cool-season grass in arid areas needs irrigation at least twice a week to keep it active in summer. Warm-season grasses may need irrigation once or twice a month to remain active in summer. Two native warm-season prairie grasses used for lawns are buffalograss and blue gramagrass.

Conserving Resources
continued

Collecting rainwater is a centuries-old dry-climate tactic.

Bearded irises thrive and bloom profusely in dry-climate gardens. Water runoff from a driveway provides needed moisture.

Make use of water on site

Water conservation in a xeriscape reduces the need to irrigate. One way to minimize supplemental watering is to use natural precipitation and other available water. Frequently abundant on-site water is wasted. Rainwater from roof structures, driveways, walks and other hard surfaces, as well as water from up-slope runoff, makes up this unused available water resource.

The goal in xeriscape is to intercept this available water for garden use before it leaves the site. There are various ways to do this.

Collect rainwater from roofs

Collect rainwater off a roof by directing downspouts into a whiskey barrel or other type of container. Think of the roof as a watershed and the gutter as the channel or river. The storage area becomes the reservoir. To convey the water from the storage to the garden, elevate the container at least a foot in order to fill a watering can or attach a hose to the storage container and conduct water directly into the garden.

Place a mesh screen at the end of each gutter and downspout to keep litter out. The storage container should also be covered with a mesh screen and lid. You can funnel roof water directly into a planted area but will need to slow and spread the runoff with an apron at the end of the downspout.

If it rains ¼ inch, the average house will yield a typical whiskey barrel full of runoff. One inch of rain for 1,000 square feet of roof harvests 623 gallons of water. You can estimate potential water provided from your roof by measuring the square feet of the roof, multiplying by 623, and then dividing by 1,000. In arid and semiarid environments, rainfall is low and variable. You should provide for overflow in order to keep water away from the foundation when you collect water. You can do this by having several storage containers and by making any soil that collects the overflow slope away from your home's foundation.

Redirect runoff from hard surfaces

You can also intercept water from patios, drives, and other paved areas by redirecting its flow to planted areas or gardens. You can channel water by creating contours or furrows to the garden or by creating basins, depressions, or saucers around plants or planting beds. To increase the water-holding capacity of the soil, you can also amend it to the depth of the root zone. Water should drain freely. In loamy soil, 1 inch of water will move through the soil about 1 foot deep.

Groundcover roots extend about 1 foot. Therefore, the swale or basin should be 1 inch deep. Tree and shrub roots can grow 2 to 3 feet; therefore, the depression should be 2 to 3 inches deep. There should be no hardpan. If you create a depression without plant coverage, fill the area with organic mulch. Water should not stand for more than 12 hours.

Direct water to planting beds. Make sure the soil is well-aerated and drains well.

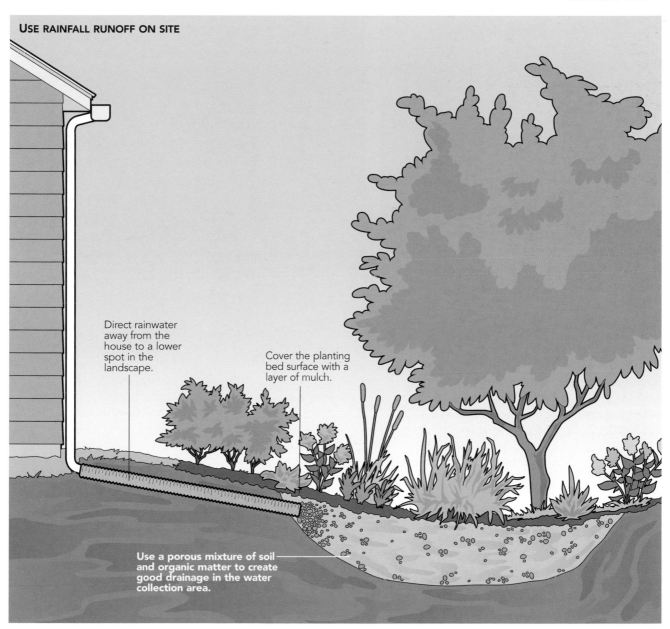

USE RAINFALL RUNOFF ON SITE

Direct rainwater away from the house to a lower spot in the landscape.

Cover the planting bed surface with a layer of mulch.

Use a porous mixture of soil and organic matter to create good drainage in the water collection area.

Conserving Resources

continued

Prevent water runoff by eliminating hard surfaces that are not porous and by creating swales where water can collect and soak into soil.

Where rainfall is precious, direct runoff to planted areas. Santa Barbara daisy (*Erigeron*) and New Zealand flax edge this rock-lined channel.

Minimize runoff

Preventing water from rapidly leaving the site is a primary goal. You can minimize runoff by reducing hard surface areas. Use porous paving materials such as brick or stone interplanted with low-growing plants, or remove hard surface areas such as paths and patios, and use mulch or other vegetation instead. Large boulders also work. Placing them strategically diverts or slows water flow. Use microclimates created by large rocks to grow accent plants that prefer cool, moist soil.

Where possible, create angles for hard surfaces to drain toward a garden. Improve water storage by amending the soil next to a hard surface and using groundcovers or organic mulch. Minimize cultivation and create windbreaks to reduce evaporation. Trees and shrubs planted in strategic locations reduce runoff and flow by intercepting rainwater.

Maximize runoff opportunities

You can maximize opportunities from the water runoff from up-slope or adjacent planting sites, such as from neighboring sprinkler systems or runoff. This allows two areas to be watered at the cost of one.

Use ET as a guide

Evapotranspiration rate (ET) is a representative number for the amount of water lost through soil evaporation and plant transpiration of a given plant (usually turfgrass). The ET rate is given in inches and presumes what turf needs on a daily or weekly basis. It is a good guide for cool-season lawns and helps you anticipate water needs for other plants. General landscape needs are approximately 60 to 80 percent of the ET rate for turf. Trees and shrubs need approximately 50 percent of the ET rate for lawns. This rate will be much lower when using xeric plants. ET rates are usually announced in a gardening section of the local newspaper or are provided by a cooperative extension office or your municipal water supplier.

Minimize waste

Xeriscape is about conserving all natural resources. Making compost and mulch not only conserve resources but also save space in landfills (see page 45). Also, when possible use recycled material for decks and other hard surfaces on your property. Reduce waste disposal by purchasing materials in bulk or with minimal packaging. Do not purchase nonrenewable organic products that damage natural ecosystems (such as mountain peat instead of peat moss harvested from northern bogs.). Avoid plastic products whenever possible. They are not biodegradable and are potentially toxic if burned. Reuse or recycle garden products. Return containers to garden centers for their reuse. Reuse to "new-use" is an effective and efficient way of recycling.

Water applied higher on a slope will collect at the base to benefit plants at the bottom.

Creating Dry Gardens

Texas sage, with its striking silver foliage, suits many dry summer gardens. Coral aloe and Spanish bayonet (*Yucca*) accent the foreground.

When settlers first came to North America, they brought with them European garden styles and a corresponding plant palette. Both were suitable to eastern North America since this part

SILVER TO GRAY WOODY PLANTS

Sand sage (*Artemisia filifolia*)
Tall sagebrush (*Artemisia tridentata*)
Four-wing saltbush (*Atriplex canescens*)
Silver butterflybush (*Buddleja alternifolia* 'Argentea')
Silverberry (*Elaeagnus commutata*)
Sea buckthorn (*Hippophae rhamnoides*)
Texas sage (*Leucophyllum frutescens*)
Willow-leaf pear (*Pyrus salicifolia*)

of the country is not unlike much of Europe in humidity and natural precipitation. As people moved westward, they kept their gardens and plants even though weather and natural environments changed. People were proud of their oasis in the "desert." This came at a cost. Gardeners had to work harder and use more resources for similar quality. Over the last 20 years, all this has been changing. People are more aware of their environment as fresh water becomes less available. Gardeners from arid environments are becoming more creative and setting new standards. They have so much to work with—interesting plants, rich yet soft color tones, dramatic plant forms, contrasting textures, open skies, and a variety of colorful stones and rocks. All these assets present opportunities for creative designs and plant introductions.

Silver and blue gardens

Plants with these foliage colors have special roles in arid gardens because most come from environments with similar growing conditions. Most need abundant sun, low relative humidity, alkaline to neutral soil, excellent drainage, and soil low in nutrients and organic matter—factors easy to find in arid lands. The biggest challenge in growing them is keeping stems, leaves, and crowns dry while providing moisture to their roots. They dislike wet soil, especially when accompanied with cool temperatures. Even though blue and silver foliage plants come from a variety of

ecosystems, many have similar needs and are easy to group together.

Although the leaves appear to be silver or blue, they are actually green. The foliage appears silver because of numerous surface hairs, or scales. Hairs keep the foliage cool and reflect sunlight. Other plants with blue foliage are hairless; their color is from a waxy bloom covering the surface. This wax keeps moisture in the leaves. Both surface hairs and wax are adaptive mechanisms for plants that grow in arid climates.

Silvery snow-in-summer (*Cerastium*) softens the edge of the walkway, while blue fescue (*Festuca*) and lamb's-ears (*Stachys*) planted in pockets on this slope make an attractive low-water landscape.

BLUE FOLIAGE TREES AND SHRUBS

Wright acacia (*Acacia wrightii*)
Chisos agave (*Agave havardiana*)
Yellow palo verde (*Cercidium microphyllum*)
Cypress selections (*Cupressus arizonica*)
Horizontal juniper (*Juniperus horizontalis* 'Blue Chip')
Banana yucca (*Yucca baccata*)

Creating Dry Gardens
continued

Echeveria setosa is suited to areas without frost, or you can grow it in containers that can be moved indoors.

There are various ways to use silver and blue foliage plants. They can be included in a mix with other dryland plants, or you can create a garden exclusively using them. The latter is based on a monochromatic scheme that includes the various hues (such as woolly gray, chalky white, silver, and silvery green). Silver foliage plants are effective with bright or clashing colors. They also help to lighten dark areas. Blue foliage gardens with monochromatic hues can introduce violet and lavender as well. Many colorful foliage plants have interesting and sometimes unusual foliage and texture. Keep these in mind when planning your garden. The combination adds interest, contrast, and appeal.

SILVER TO GRAY HERBACEOUS PLANTS

Pussy-toes *(Antennaria dioica)*

Fringed sage *(Artemisia frigida)*

Beach wormwood *(Artemisia stelleriana)*

Coronado hyssop *(Agastache aurantiaca 'Coronado')*

Curlicue sage *(Artemisia versicolor)*

Snow-in-summer *(Cerastium tomentosum)*

Hairy canary clover *(Dorycnium hirsutum)*

Licorice plant *(Helichrysum petiolare)*

Lavender *(Lavandula angustifolia)*

Russian sage *(Perovskia atriplicifolia)*

Silver sage *(Salvia argentea)*

Dusty miller *(Senecio cineraria)*

Silver buffaloberry *(Shepherdia argentea)*

Lamb's-ears *(Stachys byzantina)*

Silver speedwell *(Veronica incana)*

Soft-to-touch lamb's-ears *(Stachys byzantina)* is a rugged silver foliage plant that makes an attractive ground cover for sunny sites.

Gray and silver combination pairs everlasting *(Anaphalis)* and sage *(Artemisia)*.

Festuca 'Elijah Blue' has outstanding evergreen blue foliage and is ideal for xeric gardens.

Mediterranean native silver sage *(Salvia argentea)* has large, fuzzy, silvery leaves.

BLUE FOLIAGE HERBACEOUS PLANTS

Echeveria *(Echeveria* spp.)
Blue lyme grass *(Elymus glaucus)*
Blue fescue *(Festuca glauca)*
Blue avena *(Helictotrichon sempervirens)*
Heavy Metal switchgrass *(Panicum virgatum* 'Heavy Metal')
Burro's tail *(Sedum morganianum)*
Blue spruce sedum *(Sedum reflexum)*
Cape blanco sedum *(Sedum spathulifolium)*
Little bluestem *(Schizachyrium scoparium* 'The Blues')

Ornamental Grass Gardens

Like silver or blue foliage gardens, ornamental grasses are well suited to arid climates because they have many plants adapted to dry conditions. Unlike silver and blue foliage plants, grasses lack the variety in form and texture but still animate the garden with movement and sound. When wind travels across the landscape, grasses sway and rustle. In late afternoon, many take on a glow, becoming translucent when back lit by the setting sun. Grasses have four seasons. They emerge in spring with fresh green foliage, bear flowers and fruit in summer, turn colors in fall, and persist in full form throughout winter.

Ornamental grasses add a fine texture to landscapes which is a relief to the more common oblong-leafed plants.

Most grasses are easy to grow and maintain. They tolerate a wide variety of soils, rarely need fertilizers, have no major pests. Once a year, remove dried foliage before new growth appears. You can cut the plant back to several inches above the ground with shears or pruners, or comb out dried foliage with a hand cultivator. Generally, you should thin or divide grasses every few years if they die in the center or become too large. Their dense, fibrous root systems can be difficult and challenging, but this is also what makes them well suited to arid environments.

You can use ornamental grasses in a variety of ways. As with silver or blue foliage gardens, you can dedicate an entire area exclusively to them. They also combine well with other herbaceous and/or woody plants. Ornamental grasses are excellent in containers, along dry streams, in natural settings, and as barriers, screens, or hedges. To enhance sound and movement, plant them with enough space to give them room to move freely. If you use them as a barrier or hedge, plant them close for quicker fill in.

The best type of growth for an ornamental grass is a bunch grass. It grows in clumps rather than spreading by above- or belowground stems. If the latter growth is vigorous, the grass can be invasive. Because grasses are adaptable with the potential to seed and disperse great distances, they can be a problem in the wrong environment. When choosing an ornamental grass (or any other garden plant), select one

Ornamental grasses are well-suited to gardens in areas that were once prairie, savanna, or parklands.

Lindheimer muhly (*Muhlenbergia lindheimeri*) and gulf muhly (*M. capillaris*) are stunning Texas natives.

that does not have the tendency to become an invasive threat to natural environments in your region. At one time pampas grass escaped cultivation in several western areas, but it now outcompetes many native plant species.

Ornamental grasses are often grouped as warm- or cool-season plants. Warm-season species are slower to emerge from dormancy, flower in summer to early fall, and become fully dormant with the first fall frost. They do better under hot and dry conditions than cool-season plants and require fewer divisions over a period of years than cool-season species.

WARM-SEASON GRASSES

Lyme grass (*Elymus arenarius, E. magellanicus*)
Ravenna grass (*Erianthus ravennae*)
Hare's tail grass (*Lagurus ovatus*)
Maiden grass (*Miscanthus oligostachys, Miscanthus sinensis* and cultivars)
Switch grass (*Panicum virgatum* and cultivars)
Fountain grass (*Pennisetum alopecuroides, P. setaceum*)
Ruby grass (*Rhynchelytrum nerviglume*)
Natal grass (*Rhynchelytrum repens*)
Little bluestem (*Schizachyrium scoparium* and cultivars)
Indian grass (*Sorghastrum nutans* and cultivars)
Mexican feather grass (*Nassela tenuissima*)

Ornamental Grass Gardens *continued*

Ornamental grasses combine well with plants of the daisy family.

Cool-season grasses begin growth in early spring, flower in summer, and grow slowly with summer heat, some going fully dormant. In late summer and fall when temperatures cool, many resume activity. Various species can be kept active with supplemental water.

These grasses may require more frequent division to keep them healthy and vigorous. Otherwise many tend to die out in the center.

COOL-SEASON GRASSES

Bulbous oatgrass *(Arrhenatherum bulbosum)*
Quaking grass *(Briza media)*
Feather reed grass *(Calamagrostis acutiflora, C. arundinacea)*
Tufted fescue *(Festuca amethystina* and cultivars)
Blue fescue *(Festuca glauca* and cultivars)
Blue avena *(Helictotrichon sempervirens)*
Velvet grass *(Holcus mollis* 'Albovariegatus')
Blue hair grass *(Koeleria glauca)*

Fall color foliage and grassy textures extend seasonal interest into the winter.

Sculpture Gardens

Artistic plant form and plant texture are the basis for a sculpture garden. Unlike topiary (shaping plants through special pruning and cutting), xeric sculpture gardens are designed with naturally interesting plant shapes and forms from arid (mostly desert) regions. Dryland environments again lend themselves to this creative garden theme because drought-tolerant plants adapted to harsh environments have unique forms. Succulent species (plants that store water in stems and leaves) have lush, rounded stems and foliage; others have sharp, pointed, thrusting leaves. Both offer sculptural qualities. Many artful specimens develop colorful, wily spines and thorns. Some species cloak themselves with woolly hairs or wax. Several have unusually large stems with tiny leaves. You can choose from an abundant list of species:

AGAVE SELECTIONS: *Agave*, leaves in rosettes, thrust upward.

ALOE SELECTIONS: *Aloe*, leaves in rosettes, thrust upward.

MANZANITA SELECTIONS: *Arctostaphylos* species, shrubs with evergreen foliage arranged vertically against mahogany bark.

OLD-MAN CACTUS: *Cephalocereus senilis*, cactus covered with long, white, silky hairs.

DESERT SPOON: *Dasylirion*, leaves in rosettes, thrust upward.

HEDGEHOG CACTUS: *Echinocereus pectinatus*, cactus with band of colorful thorns.

BRITTLE BUSH: *Encelia*, leaves covered with velvety hairs.

EPHEDRA SELECTIONS: *Ephedra* species, green, leafless shrub with broomlike texture and form.

Beavertail cactus (Opuntia basilaris) is accented with the planting of moss verbena (Verbena tenuisecta).

Plants with succulent foliage, such as these aloes, have inherent sculptural qualities.

This whimsical planting combines succulents and other dry-climate plants in ceramic drain tile "containers."

FISHHOOK CACTUS: *Ferocactus wislizenii,* cactus with fishhook thorns.
OCOTILLO: *Fouquieria splendens,* small leaves, stout thorns on whiplike stems.
LIVING STONES: *Lithops* species, succulent foliage like stones or pebbles.
PRICKLY PEAR, CHOLLA: *Opuntia* species, flattened to cylindrical succulent stems with few to numerous spines.
JOJOBA: *Simmondsia chinensis,* shrub with evergreen foliage arranged vertically for minimum sun exposure.
YUCCA SELECTIONS: *Yucca* species, leaves in rosettes, thrust upward.

Houseleeks, sedums, and euphorbias combine well to create pleasing textures and form.

Prairie Gardens

Natural and ecological gardens are becoming more popular because they create a sense of wilderness in a world that is losing touch with nature. Butterfly and wildlife habitats are recognized natural gardens. A more recent trend is the prairie garden. Dominated by grass plants interspersed with wildflowers, prairie gardens provide diversity, reflect seasonal change, use existing soil, are primarily sustained with natural precipitation, give rather than take from the environment, and provide wildlife habitat. They are colorful, interesting, beautiful, xeric, and sustainable. Prairie gardens are especially suitable

Prairie gardens are recognized as natural gardens, giving and not taking from the environment.

Dominated by grasses, prairie gardens provide diversity, splashes of color, and seasonal change.

Excellent short-grass prairie plants here include blue gramagrass, purple prairie clover, and Mexican hat coneflower.

in regions where grasslands once thrived. The difficulty lies in getting them established. However, once established, they nearly care for themselves. The beauty of these gardens is that species intermix, each finding its niche.

The best location for a prairie garden is in open, rolling-to-level ground with full sun and minimal root competition from mature trees. The first step in developing the garden is to identify soil type and drainage patterns. Plant choice should be based on a mix of native grasses and wildflowers that grow with the existing soil type and drainage. This information is often available from a native plant society, native plant nurseries, cooperative extension offices, universities, and botanic gardens. Choose a reliable and responsible source for this information. This is important because many noxious weeds are inadvertently introduced to a region where they can destroy a natural ecosystem. Be aware that many prairie/meadow mixes identified for the west are generic and not specific to your region. For best establishment, sustainability, and environmental ethics, use native species only. Check your state's weed ordinance for a list of noxious weeds.

Prairie Gardens
continued

Prairie gardens create a sense of wilderness and are important wildlife habitats.

Getting started

There are four ways to establish your own prairie—each involves eliminating existing vegetation.

1. Smother existing vegetation (such as a lawn) with black plastic or newspaper and/or a thick layer of mulch. Leave the cover for several months until plant growth underneath is dead. Many noxious weeds such as Canada thistle or bindweed may persist and will need special treatment. Once the vegetation is dead, remove the mulch or cover, and rake the dead plant debris. Slit seed the prairie mix about ¼- to ½-inch-deep into the soil, or till the dried vegetation into the soil to a depth of 12 inches, and then broadcast the seeds on the surface. Slit seeding uses sharp blades to cut through stubble and create grooves in the soil for the seed. Broadcast seed is spread by hand or with a spreader on the soil surface and then lightly raked into the soil.

2. In fall turn the soil over with existing vegetation (spaded roughly) and expose plant roots to cold winter temperatures. Allow it to remain through the winter. This dries out plant roots, prevents soil erosion, and allows freezing and thawing to break up soil clods. In early spring, the plants should be dead. Till them into the soil to a depth of 12 inches (remove any thick perennial roots). Rake the soil and broadcast the seed.

3. Kill existing vegetation with an herbicide containing glyphosate. (Follow all directions on the label.) Once plants are dead (about two weeks), mow the debris to a 1- to 2-inch stubble. Slit seed into the stubble, or till the debris into the soil to a depth of 12 inches. The stubble acts as a mulch and minimizes weed problems. If you choose to till, rake the area and create a fairly uniform seedbed. Note: Tilling brings weed seeds to the surface. Avoid it if you are planting in soil that is fairly loose and not compacted. The greatest challenge in establishing a prairie is managing weeds.

4. You can also start a prairie with plants, but it is more expensive and time

If a site has been prepared, sow prairie seeds over snow. Seeds will move into the soil with snowmelt.

Hydromulching uses a slurry mix containing mulch, a binder that sticks the mix to the soil, a dye, and appropriate grass and wildflower seeds.

consuming. Advantages are that plants establish more quickly, and you can control their initial placement. For a small garden, this may work. Starting from seeds instead of plants may take three to five years for establishment and weed control.

Timing

The best time to seed outdoors is early spring before the growing season, when you can take advantage of natural precipitation. Dormant seeding between mid-October and freezing also works. Most importantly, have seeds in the soil prior to weed growth to help native plants compete for moisture and nutrients.

Blue-green dye marks a hydromulched area.

Prairie Gardens
continued

When planting a prairie garden, choose plants native to your area. Here Indian paintbrush is combined with foxtail lily, lupine, and larkspur In a tapestry of texture and color.

Selecting plants

Choose plants native to your area. Prairie gardens consist of approximately 75 to 80 percent grasses and the rest wildflowers. Seed packets or suppliers will provide information on seeding rates; in general, it is about ½ pound of grass seed plus 2 ounces of wildflower seed per 1000 square feet. You can also strategically plant subshrubs for interest and contrast. Bur oak, gambel oak, live oak, and hackberry are compatible woody plants on the periphery. The following plants represent some of many prairie species. Check with local sources before planting.

FRINGED SAGE: *Artemisia frigida*

ASTER: *Aster* species

LOCOWEED: *Astragalus* species

BUFFALOGRASS: *Buchloe dactyloides*

SIDEOATS GRAMAGRASS: *Bouteloua curtipendula*

BLUE GRAMAGRASS: *Bouteloua gracilis*

SAND DROPSEED: *Sporobolus cryptandrus*

PURPLE PRAIRIE CLOVER: *Dalea purpurea*

BLANKET FLOWER: *Gaillardia aristata*

SNAKEWEED: *Gutierrezia sarothrae*

SUNFLOWER: *Helianthus* species

GALETTA GRASS: *Hilaria jamesii*

JUNE GRASS: *Koeleria cristata*

DOTTED GAY FEATHER: *Liatris punctata*

PRICKLY PEAR CACTUS: *Opuntia polyacantha*

LOCOWEED: *Oxytropis lambertii*

WESTERN WHEAT: *Pascopyrum smithii*

MEXICAN HAT CONEFLOWER: *Ratibida columnifera*

LITTLE BLUESTEM: *Schizachyrium scoparium*

GROUNDSEL: *Senecio longilobus*

SCARLET GLOBE MALLOW: *Sphaeralcea coccinea*

NEEDLE-AND-THREAD: *Hesperostipa comata*

PRAIRIE SPIDERWORT: *Tradescantia occidentalis*

Managing your prairie

The greatest challenge to establishing a prairie is weed control. Hand removal or mowing are most effective if timely. When plants are small, differentiating between weeds and natives will be difficult. Be observant. Remove unwanted plants as soon as you are sure what they are, and do not allow them to flower and seed. Once the garden is established, you may want to mow once a year in late winter after native seeds have dispersed.

Once a prairie garden is on its way, no herbicides or fertilizers are needed. Healthy plants will discourage invading weeds although weeds from adjacent sites can move in. Prairie gardens in dry months can be potentially vulnerable to fire. Be prepared to irrigate under these conditions. For additional help maintaining your prairie, contact your native plant society or cooperative extension agent.

Prairie gardens are 75 to 80 percent grasses and the rest wildflowers.

Traditional Gardens Xeric Style

Bark is used as mulch in this vegetable garden to suppress weeds and reduce water evaporation from the soil.

Some gardens are traditional and may be difficult to transform into a xeric garden. In these traditional gardens, such as vegetable gardens, the best you can do is use water efficiently and minimize waste. Other traditional herb or Victorian gardens, however, are more easily converted to xeric gardens without compromising their theme or style.

Vegetable gardens

In a small area, vegetable gardens contain plants from the Caribbean (peppers), South America (tomatoes), India (cucumbers), and the Mediterranean (lettuce), among others. Yet, you can have a productive garden and conserve water in one space with such diverse plants. **MAKE THE MOST OF WHAT YOU HAVE:** Locate the garden where there is at least six

Water in this vegetable garden is applied only to the plants in the raised beds, diminishing growth of weeds in pathways and conserving water.

hours of sun and protection from strong wind. Vegetable gardens are productive and high yield. Therefore soil is critical. It should hold nutrients, retain moisture, and drain well. You will often need to amend your soil. If your property will not support a vegetable garden, you can use raised beds and bring in the soil you need. Raised beds are advantageous because you decide the soil you want. These beds drain well, warm up faster, can be accessible on more than one side, and, are easy to keep clean. However,

they also dry out faster and are less insulated. The latter can be mitigated with hay bales around the periphery.

It is estimated that a 144-square-foot xeric vegetable garden with loamy soil will use (roughly) six gallons of water per week. Before adding water, make use of what is on the site. Collect runoff or channel it directly to the garden. If runoff is from a downspout, you may need to slow down the flow with an apron at the end of the spout. Take into account the amount of runoff and/or any natural

precipitation received. Use a rain gauge to measure how much additional water the garden needs. Locate the gauge high enough to avoid ground splashes and potential drips from overhead structures or plants. When you use supplemental water, apply it with a low-volume, low-pressure system (such as drip or microjets) or use a soaker hose. You can also use furrow or basin irrigation. These approaches apply water directly to the soil and roots with little waste from runoff or evaporation (see page 36).

Traditional Gardens Xeric Style
continued

MINIMIZE PLANT WASTE BY COMPOSTING: Use compost to amend the soil or as mulch in the vegetable garden. Apply it 1- to 2-inches-deep. By minimizing evaporation, soil crusting, and weed competition, mulch eliminates the need to cultivate and thus retards soil evaporation. At the end of the season, you can till compost, mulch, and other plant debris into the garden. Leave the garden roughly spaded in winter with a protective mulch to prevent soil erosion and moisture loss.

Weed-barrier fabric covers planting rows; water is applied under the fabric and plants grow through spaces cut into it.

PLANT ACCORDING TO LOCAL CLIMATE: Cool-weather plants need cool weather to mature; warm-weather plants need warm weather. Start hardy, cool-weather plants early enough for them to mature before hot weather. Plant warm-weather crops when the weather warms. You can also take advantage of cool days in fall by planting in late summer or early fall. Your planting time will depend on where you live and the length of growing season (days between the last frost of spring and the first frost of fall). Make note of microclimates in your garden, as they are exceptions to the general, overall climate.

SELECT PLANTS SUITED TO YOUR SOIL AND CLIMATE: Plant breeding has advanced greatly and provides gardeners with a variety of regional choices. If you buy start-up plants, select those with well-developed root systems and purchase from reputable growers.

SPACE AND THIN PLANTS APPROPRIATELY: Do not crowd plants or they must all compete for the same moisture and nutrients. This competition will affect the quality of the plants. Weakened plants are more likely to become victims of disease or insects. Seed packets and plant labels provide directions for correct spacing.

KEEP THE PLANTS HEALTHY: Remove and dispose of diseased foliage. Stake or trellis vines (melons) or tall plants (tomatoes) to keep flowers and fruits from making soil contact. Encourage beneficial insects into your garden. Minimize pesticide use.

Straw mulch is a readily available and inexpensive vegetable garden mulch.

Traditional Gardens Xeric Style
continued

Herb gardens

Herb gardens are a natural for arid climates because many plants used in these gardens are native to dry areas of the Mediterranean region. Bay, lavender, marjoram, mint, oregano, rosemary, sage, salvia, and thyme are part of both soft and hard chaparral communities.

Many herbs tolerate poor soil, like abundant sunshine and dry air, and adapt to various well-drained soils with pH from 6.5 to 8. Herbs may be annuals, perennials, trees, or shrubs. Some herbs are considered as subshrubs (plants with herbaceous stems and a woody base). These are ideal candidates for formal border plants typical of traditional herb knot gardens (examples are lavender, rosemary, and thyme). Most plants used as herbs are deciduous, but some are evergreen (such as bay). Both adapt well to bonsai or container specimens.

Because so many herbs are native to hot and dry Mediterranean regions, gardens that feature them are naturals for similar arid environments.

CULINARY HERBS FOR XERIC GARDENS

Dill *(Anethum graveolens)*
French tarragon *(Artemisia dracunculus)*
Cilantro, coriander *(Coriandrum sativum)*
Cumin *(Cuminum cyminum)*
Sweet bay *(Laurus nobilis)*
Lemon balm *(Melissa officinalis)*
Mint *(Mentha* species)
Greek oregano *(Origanum heracleoticum)*
Sweet marjoram *(Origanum majorana)*
Italian parsley *(Petroselinum neapolitanum)*
Rosemary *(Rosmarinus officinalis)*
Common sage *(Salvia officinalis)*
Summer savory *(Satureja hortensis)*
Common thyme *(Thymus vulgaris)*

Herbs are used in culinary dishes to flavor and spice foods. Each culinary herb has its own distinct flavor and aroma. Herbs are used fresh or dry in floral arrangements, potpourri, perfumes, toiletries, and candles. Throughout history, herbs have played a major role medicinally and spiritually. In modern times, many rely on them as natural cures.

HERBS ARE ALSO ORNAMENTAL: They are used as groundcovers, in containers, in perennial flower gardens, among vegetables, or in bedding displays. Most take up little space and can be designed for formal or informal gardens. Whatever style you choose, grow herbs under drip irrigation to achieve a utilitarian, attractive, low water use garden.

Creeping thyme fills spaces between pavers of this small backyard patio.

Make a checkerboard pattern by alternating creeping thyme with patio pavers.

Dusty miller, rosemary, and santolina create interesting xeric gardens.

Victorian Gardens

Beach wormwood (*Artemisia stelleriana* 'Silver Brocade') and mealycup sage (*Salvia farinacea*) are Victorian period plants that are well-suited to xeric gardens.

Mulch generously and use drip irrigation to reduce water needed to maintain gardens of bedding plants.

In the garden, the Victorian era reflects a time when many "nature themes" were fashionable. Floral and botanical designs on fabrics, wallpaper, and rugs were simulated outdoors. Areas were accentuated with flowering vines, statues, fountains, and ornate, leafy cast-iron furniture. Victorian gardens were not subtle but were bold, dramatic, colorful, and bright. Much of this was achieved using large plants, foliage such as pampas grass or castor bean, and exotic palms and bamboo. Containers were also "in." Large urns and smaller vases were planted with geraniums, fuchsias, and agave.

Color ruled the garden, especially if it was bold. The Victorians combined brilliant orange with deep purple, fiery red with sharp blue, and yellow with white and blue together. Most notably, Victorian gardens created bedding displays. These ideas were in part transferred from intricately patterned Persian rugs. Victorian gardens decorated lawns with flowers in geometric shapes and later in sculptures of clocks, symbols, or place names.

Popular Victorian plants included ageratum, banana or bird of paradise, castor bean, Brugmansia, cockscomb, dusty miller, feverfew, geranium, lobelia, petunias, phlox, salvia, and verbena, as well as ornamental grasses. Bedding and container gardening are still popular today.

Use more xeric species, select colors that vibrate, and plan for maximum contrast in order to design your own Victorian style and still retain xeriscape ideals. Design with a punch.

XERIC PLANTS FOR VICTORIAN BEDDING

Coronation Gold yarrow *(Achillea filipendulina* 'Coronation Gold')

Desert Sunrise hyssop *(Agastache* 'Desert Sunrise')

Powis Castle silver sage *(Artemisia* 'Powis Castle')

Winecup *(Callirhoe involucrata)*

Yellow spider flower *(Cleome lutea)*

Tickseed *(Coreopsis tinctoria)*

California gold poppy *(Eschscholzia californica)*

Indian blanket flower *(Gaillardia pulchella)*

Gazania *(Gazania rigens)*

Globe amaranth *(Gomphrena globosa)*

Texas red yucca *(Hesperaloe parviflora)*

Redhot poker *(Kniphofia uvaria* 'Hybrid Mix')

Arroyo lupine *(Lupinus succulentus)*

Blackfoot daisy *(Melampodium leucanthum)*

Four-o'clock *(Mirabilis jalapa)*

Evening primrose *(Oenothera macrocarpa* 'Comanche Campfire')

Fountain Grass *(Pennisetum setaceum)*

Petunia *(Petunia* hybrids)

Desert canterbury bells *(Phacelia campanularia)*

Moss rose *(Portulaca grandiflora)*

Gloriosa daisy *(Rudbeckia hirta)*

Raspberry Delight salvia *(Salvia* ×Raspberry Delight)

Mealycup sage *(Salvia farinacea)*

Creeping zinnia *(Sanvitalia procumbens)*

Dusty miller *(Senecio cineraria)*

Marigold *(Tagetes* species)

Mexican sunflower *(Tithonia rotundifolia)*

Blue Reflection creeping speedwell *(Veronica* 'Blue Reflection')

Hummingbird plant *(Zauschneria garrettii* 'Orange Carpet')

Narrowleaf zinnia *(Zinnia angustifolia)*

Desert zinnia *(Zinnia grandiflora)*

Pearly everlasting (*Anaphalis tripinervis*) used as a cut flower is best grown under drip irrigation.

Victorian-style flowers for floral bouquets are especially easy to grow in prairie gardens.

This gravel garden features purpletop verbena (*Verbena bonariensis*), onion (*Allium*), and yarrow (*Achillea*).

PLANTS FOR
Dry Climate Gardens

IN THIS CHAPTER

Selecting the Plant
for the Site **84**

Trees **85**

Shrubs **96**

Perennials **108**

How successful a plant is within the garden depends on how well the growing site satisfies its needs. In the natural world, many plant seeds may die before even one is able to grow to maturity. It is safe to assume that millions of seeds fail for each one that succeeds. Temperature, moisture, air, and the absence of predators are necessary for a plant to grow to maturity.

Unlike nature, gardeners nurture their plants and protect them from adverse elements to reduce the chance of failure. However, if the plant is not right for the environment, it will not reach maturity no matter what the gardener does. Magnolias grown in the west cannot measure up to those grown in the southeast. When there are so many other outstanding plants that grow in arid environments, why choose one doomed to failure? This chapter lists some favorite plants for xeric gardening.

Russet buffaloberry grows well in dry shade.

Sea buckthorn grows best in sandy soil.

Selecting the plant for the site

You may choose from thousands of species of plants—each dependent on and influenced by similar factors (light, water, temperature, wind, soil, air, and land forms) to grow, survive, and reproduce. Some plants grow in sun, others require shade. You will find plants adapted to survive in dry environments and plants adapted to survive in moist or wet ones. Certain plants do better in clay soil, others in sandy or rocky soil. This listing is only a small portion of plants adapted to dry climate gardens. The focus is on plants native to the western United States, but many introduced plants will thrive in the region, too.

In each of the plant descriptions, there is reference to conditions in which a plant naturally grows. These are indicators. If you can provide similar conditions in your garden, the plant should thrive. Also listed are hardiness zones in which plants are likely to grow best. These are regions that identify average minimum winter temperatures for an area. The USDA map is used in this chapter. Because microclimates play such an important role in arid environments, you may find that your property differs from typical for your area by at least one zone. Measurements on the plant silhouettes indicate typical dimensions of the plant after 5 years for shrubs or after 20 years in the landscape for trees.

Aged piñon pine clings to a cliff in Grand Canyon National Park, Arizona.

Trees

CATCLAW ACACIA

Acacia greggii
a-KAY-sha GREG-ee-i

- Yellow flowers followed by rust-colored seedpods
- Small tree with irregular shape
- Southwestern deserts that receive less than 12 inches of rain annually
- Zones 7 to 11

15'
15'

Catclaw acacia is a rugged, deciduous, small tree or large shrub that grows 10 to 15 feet tall and wide (somewhat larger with regular moisture). Its branches are distinct because of the numerous hooked spines that look like cat claws. Its coarse winter form is tempered in summer by delicate, feathery, gray-green pinnately compound leaves. In late spring after the rains, there is a profusion of yellow, 3-inch, catkin-like flowers followed by rusty-colored, twisted 6-inch pods.

USE: Catclaw acacia makes an excellent small tree and provides filtered shade for a patio or courtyard; it also grows well in a container. The broad, flattened canopy emphasizes horizontal lines at the corner of one-story homes. In general, it is a good accent plant for desert gardens and is particularly attractive with crushed stone as mulch. Planted in mass, it makes a barrier, screen, or thicket for wildlife.

CULTURE: Catclaw acacia grows with 10 to 12 inches of rain or irrigation a year. It tolerates drought, heat, alkaline soil, and full sun, even if reflected off a nearby wall. Drought tolerant, it grows best and faster with occasional deep soakings.

Combine with creosote bush, boxthorn, desert willow, encelia, prickly pear, and globe mallow.

RELATED SPECIES: *Acacia constricta*, whitethorn acacia, is native to warm deserts. The fragrant flowers are small puffballs. It differs from catclaw acacia by its straight spines on new growth and red stems.

Acacia constricta grows well in well-drained sandy or caliche soils.

Flowers of knife acacia (*Acacia cultriformis*) bloom in February in mild winter areas. The tree is hardy to 25° F.

BIGTOOTH MAPLE

Acer grandidentatum
AY-sir grand-ee-den-TAY-tum

- Orange-red fall color
- Deciduous tree
- Warm and cold desert
- Zones 4 to 8

25'
20'

Bigtooth maple is an attractive, tidy deciduous tree—up to 40 feet—on moist sites or a large shrub (less than 15 feet) on drier sites. It is one of the few maples that tolerates heat. It has a clean, refined, variable form and displays outstanding orange-red leaf colors in fall.

USE: This is a small to medium shade tree with one or multiple stems and year-round interest. It is excellent as a large shrub combined with companion plants with similar cultural needs.

CULTURE: Bigtooth maple tolerates some shade, although fall color will be compromised. It has a wide-spreading, shallow root system and should be mulched to reduce evaporation. It tolerates both moist and dry locations and prefers soils with a pH between 6 and 8.

Combine with chokecherry, creeping hollygrape, gambel oak, jamesia, ninebark, rock spirae, serviceberry, snowberry, three-leaf or smooth sumac, and Wood's rose.

Bigtooth maple is one of the few maples that tolerates heat and alkaline soil.

Trees *continued*

Aesculus californica
ESS-kuh-luss cal-a-FOR-nick-a

The showy flowers of California buckeye appear in midspring.

CALIFORNIA BUCKEYE

- White flowers
- Deciduous tree
- California coastal sage chaparral
- Zones 7 to 10

This is a small deciduous tree or large shrub that grows 10 to 30 feet tall and wide. Attractive year-round, it has a whitish trunk; flat-topped crown; large, palmate leaves; and showy, 6-inch creamy white to pale pink, scented flowers in spring. The smooth, fig-shaped, light brown fruits with glossy brown seeds are inedible. Fruits of all buckeyes (*Aesculus*) are poisonous. However, they are very nutritious. To use them as a food source, Native Americans used to boil them first to remove the poison. They also used the seeds in streams to daze fish and make them easier to catch.

USE: California buckeye is a fine ornamental shade or specimen tree. Coarse summer and winter texture combine well with other chaparral plants.

CULTURE: This tree is native to Mediterranean climates with cool, moist winters, hot, dry summers, and less than 14 inches annual rainfall. It grows in sandy to gravelly to loamy soils with pH 4 to 8, in clay or loam, and in full sun to partial shade. Leaves develop scorch and drop when water stress becomes severe.

Combine California buckeye with California buckwheat, ceanothus, encelia, gooseberry, manzanita, mountain mahogany, and western redbud.

Celtis reticulata
SELL-tiss re-TIC-you-la-ta

Prominent veining in leaves is the source of both the specific and common name "netleaf."

NETLEAF HACKBERRY

- Orange-red fruits
- Deciduous tree
- Southwestern deserts and the Great Plains
- Zones 4 to 10

This is a small deciduous tree, sometime scraggly, 10 to 30 feet tall, though it can grow larger with moisture. The short and crooked trunk with warty projections that merge into the gray to reddish-brown bark is a particularly attractive feature. Leaves are heart-shaped with an uneven base, netted veins, and a rough sandpaper texture. Flowers are inconspicuous. Fruits are a colorful orange-red to purplish-black, and sweet tasting. Netleaf hackberry has a strong taproot as well as many shallow, lateral fibrous roots that potentially spread more than 15 feet. It is a very adaptable tree.

USE: Netleaf hackberry is excellent for moderate shade and for attracting wildlife. Plant three to five in a grove to make the garden appear more mature.

CULTURE: Netleaf hackberry grows at elevations from 2,500 to 6,000 feet where annual rainfall is between 10 and 30 inches, usually in rocky canyons, desert shrubland, open woodlands, and semiarid grasslands. Scattered trees are often found where upper-desert shrubland and semiarid grassland merge into savanna. It grows in gravelly, sandy, or loam soil with pH 7 to 8.5, preferring full sun (minimum of six hours per day), but tolerating partial shade. It grows in dry or moist soil, and is more tolerant of drought with age. It is known to grow in areas with seven inches of precipitation and summer temperatures that exceed 110° F.

In dry areas, combine this tree with Apache plume, honey mesquite, Joshua tree, juniper, piñon pine, and whitethorn acacia.

BLUE PALO VERDE

Cercidium floridum
sir-SID-ee-um floor-ID-ee-um

- ■ Blue-green bark and yellow flowers
- ■ Deciduous tree
- ■ Sonoran Desert
- ■ Zones 9 to10

This is a small, spiny tree up to 30 feet tall with thin, smooth, blue-green bark and stems. In midspring, it is covered with fragrant yellow flowers. The bark is smooth yellow-green, later becoming brown and slightly scaly. Palo verde is leafless most of the year during drought. When in leaf, the small compound foliage creates a light, airy texture. It has a very deep root system. It also is leafless most of the year.

USE: Plant blue palo verde where you can benefit from its filtered shade, or use it as a specimen tree for its winter color and graceful form. Use as a large shrub or tree.

CULTURE: Blue palo verde grows from sea level to 4,000 feet on flats, washes, steep mountain slopes, upland on hills, and mountain slopes. It is best on sandy to gravelly or coarse loamy soil that is low in nitrogen and phosphorus. Water sparingly once it is established. Because roots naturally trap their own nitrogen, it does not need additional fertilizer. Combine it with agave, buckwheat, desert willow, encelia, and hesperaloe.

RELATED SPECIES: *Cercidium microphyllum*, littleleaf palo verde, is similar but has smaller leaves.

In spring, the numerous yellow flowers of blue palo verde are particularly striking against the bright green trunk and branches.

WESTERN REDBUD

Cercis occidentalis
SIR-siss ox-a-den-TAL-us

- ■ Pink to lavender flowers followed by dark red seed pods
- ■ Small rounded tree or large shrub
- ■ California chaparral and forests
- ■ Zones 6 to 10

This is a rounded deciduous tree or shrub that grows 6 to 15 feet tall and wide. Leaves are kidney-shaped; lavender to pink flowers look like flowers of sweet peas; they're followed by reddish-purple seed pods that persist throughout the winter.

USE: Western redbud is excellent in informal, natural gardens, as a specimen, container, patio, or courtyard tree. It is truly memorable in bloom, especially when planted in groups of 3 to 5 (spaced 5 feet apart). It also serves well in gardens designed to attract birds and butterflies.

CULTURE: Western redbud is found along streambeds and rock outcroppings at elevations up to 4,500 feet. Plant it in full sun. It is tolerant of clay soil, although it is best in coarse, lean, nutrient-poor soil with a pH 5.5 to 8. Water to establish young plants and then sparingly. Too much water may encourage crown rot.

Combine with birchleaf mountain mahogany, buckwheat species, chamise, cup-leaf ceanothus, flannel shrub, greenleaf manzanita, and juniper.

RELATED SPECIES: *Cercis texensis*, Texas redbud is a variable native.

Western redbud is the west's counterpart to the popular eastern redbud of the northeast.

Trees *continued*

Cercocarpus ledifolius
SIR-co-car-pus led-a-FOL-ee-us

CURLLEAF MOUNTAIN MAHOGANY

- Dark green leaves and silver-gray bark
- Small evergreen tree or shrub
- Warm and cold deserts
- Zones 5 to 10

8'
6'

This small broadleaf evergreen tree or shrub grows 3 to 15 feet tall by 3 to 12 feet wide. Its dark green, thick, narrow foliage presents a marked contrast against the silver-gray bark. Although in the rose family, the flowers are small and inconspicuous. Fruits are tiny but interesting because of the long, feathery, slender tail that twists the seed into the ground.

USE: Use as a tough screen or an accent plant. Espalier against a stark,

bare wall, or grow as a dwarf specimen tree in a container. It is a tidy, interesting, clean plant with minimal leaf litter. It does well in hot, dry-spot gardens.

CULTURE: Curlleaf is cold, heat, and drought tolerant. Place in full sun, or it becomes gangly. It needs well-drained soil with pH 6 to 8.5, and 7 to 12 inches of moisture per year. Do not overwater. It is one of the few species in the rose family that fixes nitrogen. Combine with aster, big sagebrush, buckbrush, buckwheat, evening primrose, Indian paintbrush, juniper, manzanita, pine, and penstemon species.

RELATED SPECIES: *Cercocarpus betuloides*, birchleaf mountain mahogany, is an 8-foot-high evergreen shrub with small, hairy, wedge-shaped leaves.

Curlleaf mountain mahogany tolerates full sun even in winter.

Cupressus arizonica
koo-PRESS-us air-a-ZONE-ee-ka

ARIZONA CYPRESS

- Blue-green foliage
- Conical to broad-spreading evergreen
- Open woodlands of warm deserts and chaparral
- Zones 5 to 8

40'
25'

This cypress is an elegant, fine-textured, coniferous evergreen tree closely related and similar to juniper. It grows 25 to 60 feet tall and is somewhat conical at first, but broadens with age. Leaves are small and variable in color, but often bluish-green. Cypress bark is reddish-brown and split into elongated strips.

'Blue Ice' Arizona cypress is noted for its silver-blue foliage.

The flowers are yellow and very small. Unlike junipers, cypress cones are round and woody. Cypresses generally have a pleasing aroma. Varieties are available with more silvery foliage or a pyramidal shape.

USE: Arizona cypress is often used for a windbreak or barrier, or as a background planting. It can also be grown as a specimen or as an accent in a silver-blue theme garden. It does not thrive in Tucson and similar low-desert areas because it is at the very limit of its elevation range.

CULTURE: It is well-suited to hot, dry conditions. Irrigate young plants to get established, but do not overwater once established. It grows at elevations of 700 to 7,000 feet. Combine with pine, oak, Indian paintbrush, sagebrush, and agave.

RELATED SPECIES: *Cupressus glabra*, smooth cypress, has smooth gray bark and grows in Zones 7 to 10.

Fraxinus anomala
FRAK-sih-nus a-NOM-a-la

- Yellow fall color
- Deciduous shrub or small tree
- Native to cold deserts and open woodlands
- Zones 5 to 8

12'
6'

This deciduous shrub or small tree grows 6 to 18 feet tall and 4 to 12 feet wide. Unlike most ash trees that have compound leaves, this species has simple, undivided leaves. (This anomoly is the source of its name, *anomala*.) Leaves are 1½ to 2 inches long and 1 to 2 inches wide; they turn clear yellow in fall. For an ash, it has somewhat showy yellow flowers that appear just before the leaves. The tree form commonly has a crooked trunk and rounded crown. In winter, its stubby twigs and vertical branching pattern make it stand out.

SINGLELEAF ASH

USE: Use singleleaf ash in containers, in a courtyard, or espalier it against a bare wall to create a striking winter contrast. The tree looks good planted in groups, and it is attractive to wildlife. It is a tree of considerable merit and is likely to become better known in dry regions.

CULTURE: Singleleaf ash is commonly found in rocky areas of dry canyons or hillsides, in washes or gulches, at elevations from 3,000 to 11,000 feet of cold desert and open woodlands. It grows well on a variety of soil types, ranging from gravel to clay loam. It occurs more often on poorly developed soils with very little (0.5 to 2.0 percent) organic matter. Water needs are only 10 to 14 inches of rain or irrigation per year.

Combine with aster, ephedra, greenleaf rabbit brush, desert ceanothus, desert barberry, mountain mahogany, and three-leaf sumac.

RELATED SPECIES: *Fraxinus velutina*, velvet ash, is a larger tree, to 25 feet, with divided (pinnately compound) leaves.

Single leaf ash can be grown as a small tree or large shrub.

Juniperus osteosperma
joo-NIH-per-us os-tea-o-SPER-ma

- Yellow-green leaves and blue-brown berries
- Evergreen, multi-trunked tree
- Great Basin and piñon-juniper woodlands
- Zones 4 to 8

25'
12'

This single or multi-trunked evergreen tree has a rounded crown that tops out around 25 feet tall and 10 to 15 feet wide. It can also be grown as a large shrub. Leaves are yellow-green and scalelike. The fruits are actually cones with soft fleshy scales and look more like bluish-brown berries. They are very attractive against dark foliage in fall and winter. The bark peels in thin gray-brown strips, making the plant appear older than it is.

USE: Utah juniper provides excellent color for winter interest. Its slow

UTAH JUNIPER

growth—less than ½ inch a year—makes it a poor choice for a windscreen, but it is ideal for use in containers and rock gardens.

CULTURE: Utah juniper grows naturally on dry, rocky hillsides, at elevations from 3,000 to 8,000 feet, in full sun, well-drained, alkaline soil (pH 7.4 to 8). It is adapted to areas with 10 to 15 inches of rainfall per year.

Combine with ephedra, evening primrose, four o'clock, globe mallow, greenleaf rabbit brush, piñon pine, serviceberry, roundleaf shepherdia, and yucca.

RELATED SPECIES: *Juniperus monosperma*, one-seed juniper, is a tough evergreen of hillside grasslands, mesas, and escarpments. It tolerates dry summers and winter winds. Leaves are dark green, and seed cones are reddish- to blue-brown. Growth stops when moisture is not available.

Utah juniper usually has bluish fruits.

Unlike Utah juniper, one-seed juniper usually has several trunks at the base.

Trees *continued*

Parkinsonia aculeata
par-ken-SO-nee-a ak-you-lee-AY-ta

JERUSALEM THORN

- Green branches with yellow flowers in late spring
- Spreading deciduous tree
- Canyons and washes of warm deserts
- Zones 8 to 11

Jerusalem thorn is a deciduous tree that grows 25 feet tall by 20 feet wide. It is a graceful, spreading, sometimes weeping tree. Slender green branches are armed with stout spines up to 1 inch long. Minute leaflets give the tree a feathery appearance; they emerge after rain, fold up at night, then drop off with the midrib remaining. Eventually

Leaflets emerge after rain and shortly drop, leaving remaining stalks until they eventually fall.

these fall off too. In late spring to early summer a mass of yellow, pealike flowers appear followed by 3- to 4-inch long constricted pods.

USE: The excellent ornamental and sparse foliage make this a light shade tree for patio or courtyard, and a specimen in a spot garden. Yellow-green bark gives year-round interest. Attractive with cacti and succulents for a low-water but interesting texture garden.

CULTURE: This tree grows best in full sun in sandy or gravelly, alkaline and chalky soil. It needs only 12 inches of moisture per year and thrives in heat. Cold injury can occur when plants are young. It is a fairly fast grower with few problems. You may need to stake young trees.

Combine with acacia, creosote bush, desert holly, desert marigold, hop sage, mesquite, teddy-bear cholla, and yucca.

Pinus edulis
PYE-nuss ED-you-liss

Piñon pine needles are short, fragrant, and slightly curved.

TWO-NEEDLE PIÑON PINE

- Green needlelike leaves
- Evergreen tree
- Grasslands, deserts, and piñon-juniper open woodlands
- Zones 3 to 7

This is a small, shrubby, dense, rounded tree. The trunk usually divides close to the base. It grows 12 to 20 feet tall and 10 to 15 feet wide. The fragrant, blue-green leaves are short, stiff, and sickle-shaped. They grow two per bundle. They persist four to six years contributing to the tree's dense appearance. This tree can be differentiated from other piñons by the two leaves or needles per bundle. Single-leaf piñon has one needle per bundle; four-leaf pine has four needles per bundle. All have relatively small cones with fairly large, edible seeds.

USE: Two-needle piñon pine is slow growing and symmetrical when young but gradually becomes more irregular with age. You can train and prune this tree for uniformity, but this diminishes its unique, natural shape and is not recommended. The tree is good for making a dense screen in small gardens. Use it in rock gardens, in containers, and as a screen.

CULTURE: Two-needle piñon pine typically grows in the rocky soils of dry mountain slopes, mesas, and plateaus at elevations from 4,000 to 7,200 feet. It grows best with cold winter temperatures, and it is adaptable to most well-drained soils. It grows with 10 to 12 inches of moisture per year. Combine with ephedra, four-o'clock, globe mallow, serviceberry, one-seed juniper, and banana yucca.

RELATED SPECIES: *Pinus monophylla*, single-leaf pine, is similar but a better choice where winters are warmer.

PONDEROSA PINE

Pinus ponderosa
PYE-nuss pon-der-OH-sa

- Dark green leaves and cinnamon bark
- Tall evergreen tree
- Great Plains and coastal plains of California
- Zones 3 to 7

40'+
20'

This is a large tree that grows to 40 or more feet tall and 15 to 30 feet wide. Its shape is pyramidal when young, but it gradually opens with time, exposing cinnamon-colored, deeply furrowed bark on a fairly straight trunk. It has three needles per bundle, each 3 or more inches long, and oval cones, 3 to 6 inches long. On warm days the bark smells like citrus.

USE: Plant ponderosa pines in groves for forest effect or in a parklandlike setting with unmowed prairie or meadow cover. Also use as windbreak or living snow fence.

CULTURE: Plant in spring before buds break, in a location that receives full sun. It grows with 12 to 17 inches of moisture per year. The tree is adaptable to pH 5 to 9 and various soil types as long as they are well-drained. Do not overwater.

Combine with Arizona fescue, bitterbrush, blanket flower, blue grama, blue flax, common manzanita, snowberry ninebark, Rocky Mountain juniper, and roundleaf bluebells.

RELATED SPECIES: *Pinus jeffreyii*, Jeffrey pine, is similar to ponderosa pine but has blue-green needles and larger, 6- to 9-inch-long cones. It grows from southern Oregon to lower California, from 5,000 to 10,000 feet, occupying edges of moist, high mountain meadows to arid slopes bordering deserts.

Jeffrey pine grows in most conditions, tolerates heat and drought, but becomes sensitive to smog as it ages. Although a large tree, it is popular in bonsai work.

Its bark is noted for a vanilla fragrance that distinguishes it from ponderosa pine. Both Jeffrey and ponderosa pines are transitional trees between arid foothills and moist, conifer forests.

Mature ponderosa pine bark is cinnamon-colored with deep furrows.

Trees *continued*

TEXAS HONEY MESQUITE

Prosopis glandulosa
pro-SOAP-is glan-dew-LOW-sa

Dense clusters of white flowers cloak this Texas honey mesquite.

- Dark green leaves and small white flowers
- Deciduous small tree
- Common to southwestern deserts
- Zones 7 to 11

This rugged deciduous small tree or large shrub grows up to 20 feet tall. A picturesque, gnarled plant with thorny branches and fine-textured leaves, it produces sweet-smelling, whitish flowers and 4- to 9-inch pods with large, edible seeds. Species vary greatly from area to area.

USE: Slow in the beginning, the established trees may grow 2 feet per year. Deep roots keep them drought tolerant and allow them to be planted near buildings and paved areas without causing structural damage. Can grow as hedge or screen. Thorns make it a good barrier plant: space 10 feet apart. Prune it into a small shade tree or grow in a container as a specimen plant. Utilize the extensive root system of Texas honey mesquite to control soil erosion on steep hillside or to limit blowing sand.

CULTURE: Texas honey mesquite is normally found at elevations from 2,000 to 6,000 feet, in hot, dry areas in full sun. It is often found in dense thickets near desert washes or at the base of sand dunes and other areas where the water table is not far below the surface. Roots absorb nitrogen from the air allowing the tree to thrive in otherwise infertile soils. Plant during warm weather, and water intermittently to establish. Once the tree reaches the size and form you desire, stop watering except in an extreme, prolonged dry spell. Combine with catclaw acacia, creosote bush, desert holly, hop sage, Joshua tree, Mojave yucca, teddy-bear cholla, and saltbush.

RELATED SPECIES: *Prosopis juliflora*, velvet mesquite, young foliage and fruits covered with short, velvety hairs.

COAST LIVE OAK

Quercus agrifolia
KWER-kuss ag-ri-FOH-lee-ah

Coast live oak has dark green, hollylike leaves and heavy limbs.

- Dark green leaves, gray bark, golden stringlike flowers
- Broadly spreading evergreen tree
- Foothills and valleys of California's coastal ranges from northern California to Baja
- Zones 8 to 11

This is perhaps the most common broadleaf evergreen tree in California. It is large and has gnarled branches and a dense crown. The trunk often divides into upright or wide-spreading branches close to the ground. Leaves are dark green, tough, and hard. Sudden Oak Death, a fungal disease, is currently killing many trees on the Pacific Coast.

USE: It thrives along the coast and is tolerant of salt spray. Excellent for a savanna garden with mixed prairie as cover, it is also a good shade tree for a large space where it has room to spread. It can be sheared to a 12-foot hedge. Interior live oak (*Q. wislizenii*), blue oak (*Q. douglasii*), and Texas live oak (*Q. virginiana*) also lend themselves to savanna gardens.

CULTURE: Coast live oak is found naturally on moderately dry sites and is common to chaparral and open woodlands of California's Central Valley, up to 4,200 feet in elevation.

Combine with aster, blue wildrye, ceanothus, sagebrush, chamise, coyote bush, fuchsia, flowering gooseberry, hummingbird sage, June grass, manzanita, sagebrush, and slender needle grass.

GAMBEL OAK

Quercus gambelii
KWER-kuss gam-BELL-ee-i

- Dark green leaves fading to yellow in fall
- Deciduous tree
- Cold deserts and open woodlands
- Zones 3 to 9

This deciduous tree or shrub is usually found in dense groves with pine and juniper. It has deeply lobed, dark green foliage with somewhat coarse texture which turns russet to yellow-brown in fall. It naturally occurs as patches of shrubs 3 to 20 feet tall or as dispersed trees up to 30 feet tall by 15 feet wide. Patches are clones, and are therefore uniform in character and color.

USE: It is a small, informal tree or shrub best used in groups as a barrier, screen, or background for other plantings. Because of its small size and adaptability, it is one of the most versatile oaks for xeric gardens. It grows with many stems or a single trunk. Once established, it will need minimal water to keep it small and shrubby. Spacing for barriers or forest should be 6 to 8 feet apart. On the other hand, with additional moisture gambel oak can become a 25- to 30-foot tree. It also naturalizes well and provides good habitat for wildlife (urban and indigenous). Acorns are a food source for ravens, jays, squirrels, and many migratory birds.

Gambel oak is susceptible to galls produced on the leaves or stems. Small flies or wasps lay their eggs and cause the plant to form a growth where the insect matures. The galls on leaves are not harmful to the oak. Sometimes the gall on the twigs may prevent water uptake and the twig can die. By being observant, you can remove young galls to prevent problems.

Some gambel oaks have red to orange fall color, others are brown. To select those with good color, choose them in fall since there are no cultivars available of this species. There are some hybrid oaks being produced by nurseries. Most are crosses with bur oak (a larger, deciduous species popular as a shade tree).

CULTURE: Gambel oak grows naturally in well-drained, usually gravelly soil at elevations from 3,000 to 9,000 feet. It needs 12 to 15 inches of rainfall a year and will not grow where rainfall is less than 10 inches a year or where subfreezing temperatures persist for long periods. Gambel oak withstands drought because of its deep roots, thick leaves, and efficient water transport. Once established, it may not need irrigation. However, the more moisture, the larger the plant. It grows best in full sun to partial shade in well-drained soil, pH 7 to 8.5. Remove suckers to enhance tree form.

Combine with bigtooth maple, big sagebrush, creeping hollygrape, piñon or ponderosa pine, Rocky Mountain juniper, sulfur flower, three-leaf sumac, wax currant, aster, blue grama, fringed sage, globe mallow, lupine, smooth sumac, and western wheatgrass.

Gambel oak typically forms a dense thicket on dry sites and a large shrub or small tree where more moisture is available.

Trees *continued*

Sapindus drummondii
SAP-in-dus druh-MAHND-ee-i

WESTERN SOAPBERRY

- Green-white flowers in spring, amber fruits in summer, and golden leaves in fall
- Low branching, deciduous tree
- Sonoran and Chihuahuan deserts
- Zones 6 to 8

This is a single-stem to low-branched, deciduous small tree that grows 20 to 30 feet tall and is often broader than high. A truly four-season plant, its lustrous green leaves are similar to pecan leaves. Greenish-white, 6- to 9-inch flower panicles come in late spring and are followed by clusters of amber, berrylike fruits in late summer. Finally, leaves are reliably golden

Soapberry fruits are light orange to yellow-brown in loose, grape-like clusters.

in fall. In winter, the persistent ripened fruit and exfoliating bark are attractive. The fruits are rich in saponins and used for laundry soap in Mexico.

USE: It is a desirable specimen shade tree for a hot, dry site and very attractive when planted in groups. Grow with upright, loose groundcover underneath to capture and hide falling fruits.

CULTURE: It grows along waterways, canyon sides, oak woodlands, and deserts, in limestone and sandstone soils, at elevations from 2,500 to 6,000 feet. It tolerates dry soil and has no serious pests or diseases. It grows at a moderate pace and is long-lived.

Combine with burrobrush, three-leaf sumac, Indian currant, coralberry, encelia, hop bush, netleaf hackberry, Texas mulberry, and Arizona black walnut.

Sophora secundiflora
so-FOR-a see-KUND-i-flor-a

MESCAL BEAN, TEXAS MOUNTAIN LAUREL

- Dark green leaves, pale purple flowers, and orange seeds
- Evergreen tree
- Chihuahuan desert tree common to the mountains of western Texas, southern New Mexico, and adjacent Mexico
- Zones 7 to 10

Mescal bean is an evergreen tree or small shrub that grows up to 20 feet tall or is easily kept to as low as 6 feet. It has upright branches, velvety twigs, and thick green leaves. Most spectacular are the clusters of pale purple, pealike flowers that smell

In late winter to early spring, clusters of purple flowers are sweetly fragrant of grape drink.

like grape juice, and bright orange seeds that emerge from aging pods. The seeds are poisonous.

USE: It is an excellent container plant or small tree in a spot garden or courtyard. It can also be used in groupings or as an informal screen. Locate it near an entrance to enjoy the fragrant flowers.

CULTURE: The tree thrives in limestone soils, usually as scattered plants in canyons, not in clusters. It is found on slopes and along cliffs in savannas, desert grassland, and chaparrals. Plant it during cool weather in well-drained, alkaline to neutral soil in full sun or light shade. Container plants are slow to establish. It needs minimal irrigation.

Combine with *Brickellia*, desert barberry, desert willow, evergreen sumac, honey mesquite, live oak, piñon pine, and netleaf hackberry.

Washingtonia filifera
wash-ing-TONE-ee-a fee-LEAF-er-a

CALIFORNIA FAN PALM

- Bright green fronds and tan, unbranched trunk
- Tall palm with fan-shaped leaves
- Warm deserts at elevations below 3,500 feet
- Zones 7 to 10

40'
15'

California fan palm is a large palm tree with fan-shaped foliage at the top of a cylindrical, unbranched, stout trunk. It stretches up slowly until it reaches 20 to 40 feet tall. Above that, a dense head spreads 15 feet or more wide. Leaves are gray-green and very stiff. Older leaves droop around the trunk to form a skirt of dried leaves. (The California strain retains leaves while the Arizona strain naturally drops old leaves.) During the summer, streamers of white flowers emerge from the crown.

USE: Use as a strong vertical accent plant for large properties, in groups or in rows.

CULTURE: California fan palm is an indicator species, naturally growing where there is year-round surface water from seeps, springs, and streams. Grow it in full sun. It is adaptable to most soil types and high pH. It grows with 3 to 12 inches of moisture and extreme temperatures from 13° to 125° F.

Combine with alkali sacaton, California sycamore, desert holly, palo verde, saltgrass, and mesquite.

RELATED SPECIES: *Washingtonia robusta,* Mexican fan palm, and *Chamaerops humilis,* Mediterranean fan palm.

California fan palm leaves grow up to 6 feet across.

Yucca brevifolia
YOU-ka bree-va-FOH-lee-a

JOSHUA TREE

- Green, swordlike leaves and green-white flowers
- Unique treelike habit
- Mojave desert; higher slopes of warm deserts
- Zones 7 to 10

15'
10'

Joshua tree is a slow-growing, picturesque evergreen tree most associated with the Mojave desert. The leaves are evergreen, stiff and daggerlike, bunched at the end of each branch. The tips are sharply pointed and edged with fine teeth. Its branches are erect or spreading and form a dense, compact head. Greenish-white flowers are arranged in showy panicles, blooming late winter or early spring. Fruits are fleshy at first and then dry, becoming reddish and then brown.

They drop soon after they mature.

USE: It is an excellent accent or specimen plant, particularly for its sculptural qualities, and is effective in gardens designed around strongly textured plants.

CULTURE: This plant grows naturally on higher slopes of warm deserts, at elevations from 2,000 to 6,500 feet, higher than creosote bush and lower than piñon-juniper open woodlands. It grows best in full sun and in coarse to sandy loam soil. Good drainage is essential. The trunk is usually very slow to form; the plant may need support until roots establish. Roots might also need occasional supplemental water in areas with less than 5 inches of annual precipitation.

Combine with broom snakeweed, bush muhly, California buckwheat, catclaw acacia, desert sage, galleta grass, Nevada ephedra, oak species, orange poppy, and sand verbena.

Long-lived Joshua trees bring extraordinary sculptural form to a warm desert garden.

Shrubs

LECHUGUILLA

Agave lechuguilla
a-GAH-vee lay-chew-GHEE-uh

Lechuguilla is an indicator plant of the Chihuahuan Desert.

- Purple-yellow flowers on tall stalks
- Upright, spiny leaves growing from clump
- Common throughout the Chihuahuan desert
- Zones 9 to 11

This is a perennial, succulent, leafy evergreen shrub. Leaves are upright, sharply pointed, light green to yellow-green, 10 to 20 inches long. Often, lechuguilla grows in colonies with numerous rosettes produced by offsets from short underground stems. The species has fibrous shallow roots generally in the upper 5 inches of soil. The individual rosettes flower once and die. Flower stalks can be 8 to 10 feet tall. Flowers are yellow to light purple and clustered along the central stem.

USE: Agaves in general have striking form and are fairly tolerant to cold, heat, sun, drought, and poor or alkaline soil. Their sizes vary from 1 to 6 feet with many interesting leaf and color variations. Fleshy pointed leaves are usually spiny at the tip. New growth and flower stalks come from the center where water is captured. This shrub can be very dramatic with many species and varieties available to meet your needs.

CULTURE: An indicator plant of the Chihuahuan Desert, lechuguilla grows in grasslands, chaparral, and piñon-juniper woodlands, from 970 to nearly 6,000 feet. It grows in sandy or clay loam soils with an alkaline pH from 7.5 to 9. It does best in full sun but will take light shade. It grows with less than 10 inches of moisture. Do not overwater and do not mulch with organic materials—both can cause rot. Combine with alligator or one-seed juniper, beargrass, cacti, dasylirion, grama and threeawn grasses, ocotillo, piñon pine, and yucca.

SASKATOON, WESTERN SERVICEBERRY

Amelanchier alnifolia
ah-mih-LAN-kee-er al-nee-FOHL-ee-a

Saskatoon fall color.

Saskatoon flowers are fragrant, emerging right before leaves open.

- White flowers in spring, dark berries in summer, and orange leaves in fall
- Deciduous shrub
- Open woodlands and shrub communities of the Great Basin and Great Plains
- Zones 3 to 6

Saskatoon is a deciduous, variable shrub that grows 3 to 20 feet high either singly, in groups, or sometimes in dense thickets. Saskatoon is a four-season plant. In early spring, white fragrant flowers emerge. Soon after, leaves begin to grow. These small applelike, edible red to black fruits ripen about two months later. Fall colors vary from yellow to shades of orange. Winter form is clean with upright, fairly straight stems.

USE: It is an excellent ornamental to use as background to a perennial garden, to naturalize your garden, and to attract wildlife. The fruits are edible and can be used in pastries, jelly, or syrup. Several cultivars of Saskatoon serviceberry are available.

CULTURE: This plant grows naturally in canyons, on hillsides and rock outcrops, in chaparral and sage shrublands, and in parklands, at elevations from 5,000 to 10,000 feet.

It does best in full sun to moderate shade and adapts to a variety of soil types, from relatively nonfertile to nutrient-rich, pH 6 to 8. It grows in moist to dry soil but is not tolerant of prolonged drought. It needs 12 to 15 inches per year and can grow in full sun to moderate shade.

Combine with antelope bitterbrush, creeping hollygrape, fescue species, big sagebrush, bluebunch and western wheatgrass, gambel oak, gramagrass, mountain mahogany, and snowberry.

SILVER LEAD PLANT

Amorpha canescens
a-MORE-fa ka-NES-enz

- Purple flowers
- Low-growing, woody shrub
- Great Plains
- Zones 4 to 7

This is a small perennial shrub 1 to 3 feet tall with upright stems, pinnately compound downy leaves, and spikes of festive purple flowers. Outstanding during the growing season, it often dies back almost to the ground in winter.

USE: It is excellent for a dryland perennial garden, in a prairie landscape scattered among grasses, or in large groupings. It is valuable to control erosion because of its deep, extensive root system.

CULTURE: It does best in sandy to silty soil, pH 6.5 to 8.5, in full sun. Avoid heavy clay. Like other legumes, it extracts nitrogen from the air, making additional fertilizers unnecessary. Very drought tolerant, it grows with only 12 inches of precipitation, although it does well with more. It does not transplant successfully once established and should be pruned back in fall. Do not use for warm-desert area.

Combine with blue gramagrass, bur and post oak, fringed sage, inland ceanothus, little bluestem, needle-and-thread grass, prairie sandreed, prairie rose, plains prickly pear, ponderosa pine, smooth sumac, snowberry, and wax currant.

Silver lead plant provides impressive, long-lasting purple flowers against grayish-green foliage.

GREENLEAF MANZANITA

Arctostaphylos patula
ark-toe-STAFF-i-los PAT-you-la

- Small pink-white flowers in spring
- Broadleaf evergreen shrub
- Chaparral, open woodlands, parklands, and desert
- Zones 4 to 6

Greenleaf manzanita is a broadleaf evergreen shrub that grows 3 to 9 feet tall and 3 to 12 feet wide. Pink to white bell-shaped, drooping flowers in spring are followed by reddish-brown, berrylike fruit. The leaves are thick, bright green to yellow-green, and leathery. They form an imposing contrast with the rusty brown, smooth, artistically arranged branches. Older stems shred and eventually expose light-colored wood. There is much to appreciate in this one plant.

USE: It is excellent in masses, on a hillside, or at the base of needled evergreen trees. Allow it to sprawl as a groundcover. Colors are shown off effectively when planted so sunlight can be used as a backlight.

CULTURE: Grow in full sunlight on well-drained, sandy to silty loam soil, pH 5 to 7, usually at elevations from 3,100 to 10,000 feet. There are other manzanitas (such as parry, pointleaf, and pinemat manzanitas) that may be better suited for your region.

Combine with birchleaf mountain mahogany, buckwheat species, chamise, cup-leaf ceanothus, big and silver sage, Jeffrey and ponderosa pine, and penstemon species.

RELATED SPECIES: *Arctostaphylos pungens*, pointleaf manzanita from warm and cold deserts, is a widely distributed, 5- to 7-foot-high shrub. It tolerates alkaline soil, sand, and clay.

Manzanita foliage grows in a vertical plane as an adaptive method for arid environments.

Shrubs *continued*

Artemisia tridentata (syn.
Seriphidium tridentatum)
are-tah-MEES-ee-a tri-den-TAH-ta

BIG SAGEBRUSH

- Silver-gray leaves
- Erect, evergreen—
  evergray—shrub
- Very common throughout
  western North America
- Zones 4 to 9

Big sagebrush grows 3 to 10 feet tall and 3 to 6 feet wide. Larger plants usually occur where moisture is more plentiful. Flowers are yellow, very small, and grouped in dense clusters at the top of the shrub. They are not ornamental. Foliage is silver-gray because of dense whitish hairs. Simple, wedge-shaped leaves have three lobes at the tips. They contain oils which produce a distinctive aroma when crushed.

USE: It is best used informally or in naturalized gardens. Its silver-gray foliage lends itself to imaginative color gardens of contrast (orange, pink, and blue) or monochromatic themes with silver, white, and gray.

CULTURE: Big sagebrush is a component of desert shrub, chaparral, piñon-juniper woodlands, and grassland communities, at elevations from 100 to 7,000 feet. It grows well in full sun in sandy or rich, fertile soil, pH 6 to 8. Good drainage is most important. One of the few species of this family that fixes nitrogen, it does not need added fertilization and grows with 10 to 18 inches of precipitation per year. Root systems extract moisture from shallow and deeper levels of the soil profile, making them competitive with dryland grasses and wildflowers.

Combine with aster, evening primrose, juniper, manzanita, mountain mahogany, needle grass, paintbrush, penstemon, pine, rabbit brush, saltbush, snakeweed, and western wheatgrass.

An evergray shrub, big sagebrush is an important wildlife plant.

Atriplex canescens
AH-tri-plex cah-NES-enz

FOUR-WING SALTBUSH

- Light gray to silver leaves
- Evergreen shrub
- Great Plains; cold and
  warm deserts
- Zones 3 to 10

An upright, warm-season evergreen shrub, it ranges from 3 to 6 feet tall and 4 to 8 feet wide. Its growth form varies from an open, loose canopy to a dense, tight, more formal one. Its simple leaves are light gray but become lighter if the plant absorbs and deposits salts from soil through its leaf pores. Leaves also change under drought stress, turning from gray to white or silver. Flowers are small and uninteresting, but dried four-winged fruits (on female plants) are engaging while their color transforms from green to pinkish to tan. They are excellent in dried floral arrangements.

USE: This is an informal plant used alone, in groups, or as a hedge and is good on slopes and in naturalized plantings. It is an excellent container plant. Use in hot, bright areas with reflected light. Grow where foliage can receive backlight.

CULTURE: Found in sage, desert, chaparral shrubland, and grassland communities, at elevations from 150 to 7,000 feet. It occurs on sand dunes, in gravelly washes, on mesas, ridges, alluvial plains, and slopes, and is adapted to dry, saline, alkaline soil and heavy clay. It survives on 3 inches of annual rainfall and does best in full sun. Water until established.

Combine with black greasewood, black sagebrush, broom snakeweed, dropseed species, gramagrasses, juniper, piñon pine, rubber rabbit brush, western wheatgrass, and winterfat.

Excellent for wildlife, fourwing saltbush grows in full sun and adapts to a wide range of soil.

DESERT CEANOTHUS, CUP-LEAF CEANOTHUS

Ceanothus greggii
see-a-NO-thus GREG-ee-i

- Light blue flowers and dark green leaves
- Evergreen shrub
- Warm and cold deserts, chaparral, woodlands, and pine parklands
- Zones 8 to 10

This shrub may have an upright or rounded form and grows alone or in impenetrable, dense stands. Its leaves are dark green, thick, and firm, set against light gray, smooth, rigid stems. Small bluish-white flowers grouped in dense panicles cover most of the plant when in bloom. Form and flower are highly variable depending on region.

USE: This outstanding ornamental flowering shrub is used as a foundation planting, espaliered on bare walls, displayed as a specimen or in a container, and used as a groundcover. Many cultivars and hybrids of this species have been selected for flower color and form.

CULTURE: Desert ceanothus grows in warm and cold deserts among chaparral and desert shrub communities, piñon-juniper woodlands, and ponderosa pine parklands. It is adapted to a variety of soil types and tolerant of both alkaline and acidic soils. Roots tend to grow in the top 12 inches of soil, meaning evaporation-reducing mulches are particularly beneficial. Desert ceanothus roots are able to fix atmospheric nitrogen, which reduces the need for fertilizer. Plant it in full sun in well-drained sites.

Combine with California buckwheat, chamise, chaparral yucca, cliff rose, flannel bush, manzanita, mountain mahogany, oak species, silk tassel, and sumac.

Ceanothus is a versatile plant and works well in the garden, in a container, or trained as an espalier.

FERNBUSH

Chamaebatiaria millefolium
kam-e-ba-TEE-a-re-a mil-le-FO-li-um

- White flowers in spring
- Dense shrub
- Desert scrub, sagebrush, open woodlands of warm and cold deserts
- Zones 4 to 7

Once classified as a spirea, this is a densely branched, nearly evergreen, aromatic shrub. It is rounded to vase-shaped, 3 to 6 feet tall and 4 to 5 feet wide. Foliage is grayish-green and deeply dissected similar to yarrow. In spring, this unconventional plant surprises you with beautiful panicles of white flowers. In the cold desert, Native Americans make tea from the leaves to alleviate cramps and stomach pains. It is a very hardy shrub.

USE: This informal plant is effective for naturalized gardens, as a container plant, or as background for dryland, perennial gardens. It is a good choice for texture or sensory theme gardens.

CULTURE: Fernbush is found in dry, rocky, usually limestone soil, in desert scrub, sagebrush, open woodlands and parklands of warm and cold deserts, at elevations from 3,000 to 10,000 feet. It does best in full sun in a variety of soils but needs good drainage. It grows with less than 12 inches of precipitation per year.

Combine with Arizona fescue, banana yucca, blue gramagrass, cliff rose, Fremont barberry, green ephedra, ocean-spray, prairie June grass, rabbit brush, Saskatoon serviceberry, single-leaf piñon, Utah juniper, and wax currant.

Fernbush has fragrant, fernlike foliage and numerous white flowers.

Shrubs *continued*

Chilopsis linearis
kye-LOP-sis lin-ee-AIR-iss

DESERT WILLOW

- Purple flowers in summer
- Deciduous shrub or small tree
- Washes and arroyos of warm deserts
- Zones 6 to 10

Desert willow is a deciduous large shrub to small tree, 10 to 25 feet tall by 10 to 15 feet wide. It has an open, rounded crown and is usually multi-stemmed with characteristic gnarled growth. Bright green, willowlike foliage provides airy, light texture in late spring. Large, orchidlike flowers in clusters, deep purple to pink to white with yellow throats bloom

Purple and pink flowers grace desert willow in summer. It can be pruned to create a weeping willow effect.

throughout summer. It attracts hummingbirds and has long, slender, cigarlike fruit capsules.

USE: Plant as an airy accent or background. Use to filter winds or as a screen. It is attractive in mass. Under irrigation, it grows rapidly, blooming within 18 months from seed.

CULTURE: It thrives at elevations from 1,500 to 5,000 feet and loves heat, sun, or light shade. It tolerates moist soil as long as it is well-drained, pH 6 to 9, and responds quickly to summer rains and irrigation. Water deeply and infrequently. It may grow 1 to 3 feet in a month. It responds well to nitrogen but do not fertilize when mature. Remove suckers to accentuate shape of mature tree. May suffer frost damage. Combine with boxthorn, catclaw acacia, encelia, globe mallow, palo verde, and prickly pear.

Chrysothamnus viscidiflorus
cry-so-THAM-nus vis-kid-ee-FLOR-us

GREEN RABBITBRUSH

- Yellow flowers in late summer
- Low, dense shrub
- Common through warm and cold deserts
- Zones 4 to 9

This deciduous, rounded, upright shrub with many brittle stems grows 2 to 4 feet tall by 1 to 2 feet wide. Its leaves are narrow, hairless, sticky, and bright green. Golden yellow disk flowers bloom in late summer. Stems and flowers are also somewhat sticky to touch.

USE: This is a nice garden addition for its bright green foliage and late summer blooms. Use in a perennial garden, naturalize in a meadow, group in a shrub border, or grow

Unlike green rabbit brush, *Chrysothamnus nauseosus* has white felt wool on stems.

in a container. Its bright green foliage contrasts well with the grayish colors of many dryland plants. There are many other species for your garden, ranging in height from 1 to 6 feet, in colors from blue to silver-gray to gray-green.

CULTURE: It is widely distributed in cold and warm deserts, the Great Plains, desert and sage scrub, chaparral, pine parkland, and open woodlands. Grow in full sun in well-drained soil, pH 7 to 8.5. It tolerates some salt and grows with less than 12 inches precipitation per year.

Combine with big sagebrush, globe mallow, juniper, piñon, shadscale, snakeweed, and winterfat.

RELATED SPECIES: *Chrysothamnus nauseosus*, rubber rabbit brush, is a highly variable, semiwoody shrub 1 to 6 feet tall with green to blue foliage. Whitish hairs cover the stems; foliage may or may not have hairs.

Cowania mexicana stansburiana (syn. *Purshia stansburiana*)
cow-AN-ee-a mex-a-CAN-a stanz-bur-ee-AN-uh

- Light yellow flowers in late spring
- Evergreen shrub
- Cold and warm deserts
- Zones 4 to 8

Cliff rose is an evergreen shrub 3 to 8 (or more) feet tall by 3 to 5 feet wide. It has an upright, vase-shaped, open form with reddish, shreddy bark. Small, dark green, resinous leaves crowd at ends of short twigs. In late spring, it has numerous clove-scented, creamy yellow flowers, each like a miniature rose. It is a good cut flower. The ornamental fruits with tiny seeds are attached to a feathery style. When backlit, they appear translucent.
USE: An ornamental shrub for informal or naturalized garden,

CLIFF ROSE

use evergreen as a foundation plant or a hedge. It also tolerates sheering and is a good as specimen or accent in a container.

CULTURE: Cliff rose grows naturally in cold and warm deserts, chaparral, and open woodland communities, at elevations from 3,000 to 8,000 feet. The plant prefers full sun in gravelly or rocky, well-drained soil that is not too rich. It grows naturally with 10 to 25 inches of precipitation. In the garden, too much water will produce a gangly form. The plant may not need supplemental water even during prolonged droughts once established. Fertilize sparingly.

Combine with alligator and Utah juniper, Apache plume, cholla, creeping hollygrape, curlleaf mountain mahogany, fernbush, piñon pine, prickly pear species, shrub live oak, squaw apple, or threeawn grass.

Small evergreen leaves of cliff rose have been used for tea.

Dodonaea viscosa
doe-do-NAY-a vis-COS-a

- Glossy green leaves; inconspicuous white flowers
- Upright evergreen shrub
- Warm deserts, in washes and canyons
- Zones 8 to 10

Reddish-brown flaky bark contrasts with long, narrow leaves that are glossy green on upper surface. Greenish-white, inconspicuous flowers are followed by interesting three-winged, pinkish to tan, papery fruits. They are a nice contrast with the lustrous foliage. Male and female flowers usually grow on separate plants and both are needed for fruit.
USE: Train for small patio tree, grow in container, or use as informal hedge or background border to

HOPBUSH

perennial garden. Fruits may be used in dried floral arrangements.
CULTURE: Hopbush is a warm desert plant that grows in washes, canyons, and rocky to gravelly slopes, at elevations from 2,000 to 4,000 feet. It adapts to a variety of soils—alkaline and slightly acidic—as long

as there is good drainage. It is best in full sun to partial shade. Some supplemental irrigation may improve its ornamental qualities, though it usually has low water needs.

Combine with encelia, ironwood, catclaw acacia, caesalpinia, ocotillo, desert willow, and honey mesquite.

Seeds of hopbush are enclosed in a three-winged, papery fruit.

Shrubs *continued*

Ephedra viridis
ee-FED-ra vir-ID-iss

Ephedra viridis needs exceptionally well-drained soil but is outstanding once established.

GREEN EPHEDRA

- Golden flowers; tiny, bright green leaves
- Erect to sprawling leafless shrub
- Great Basin deserts
- Zones 4 to 8

This erect to sprawling, mostly leafless shrub grows 2 to 5 feet tall by 3 to 5 feet wide. The sparse, bright green, tiny, scalelike leaves are nearly invisible against the same color green stems. Numerous parallel stems with clustered branchlets point upward, resembling a broom. Golden flowers are borne in pairs along the nodes. Male and female flowers are on separate plants.

USE: The broomlike appearance of this shrub makes it perfect for a container, a rock garden, an accent or specimen, massed, or in combination with other colorful winter deciduous plants.

CULTURE: Green ephedra is a major component of the Great Basin and less so in the warm deserts. It is found in desert and sagebrush scrub, chaparral, open woodlands, and desert grassland communities, in sandy or rocky soil, at elevations from 3,000 to 7,500 feet.

This slow-growing shrub does best in full sun and well-drained soils. Cold hardy and drought tolerant, it grows with less than 8 inches of annual precipitation. There is no need for supplemental water after establishment except in prolonged drought.

Combine with big and black sagebrush, creosote bush, four-wing saltbush, galleta grass, littleleaf mountain mahogany, morning glory, sand dropseed, shadscale, Utah juniper, and Utah serviceberry.

Fallugia paradoxa
fah-LEW-gee-uh pair-uh-DOK-suh

Apache plume is named for the feathery fruit structures that resemble an Apache headdress.

APACHE PLUME

- White flowers attractive in many seasons
- Deciduous to partially evergreen shrub
- Warm and cold deserts, especially along waterways
- Zones 4 to 10

Apache plume is a deciduous to evergreen shrub (depending on moisture or temperature) with upright arching stems and grows 2 to 8 feet tall by 3 to 6 feet wide. Attractive year round, it has small, finely divided, grayish-green leaves; single, white flowers like a rose; small fruits with pinkish, feathery, elongated styles; and white, slender branchlets that become shreddy with age. Its flowers and fruit last all summer.

USE: Use as a plant for dry gardens or informally with ornamental grasses and wildflowers such as evening primroses. It looks good massed in groups of 3 to 5 plants. Also use it in decorative, colorful containers or in a spot garden as a specimen. It is also effective among large boulders in a rock garden or combined with plants that have colorful winter stems.

CULTURE: This shrub is native to warm and cold deserts along waterways and plains in dry, coarse soil. It is found in Joshua tree and piñon-juniper woodlands, at elevations from 3,000 to 9,000 feet.

It grows best in well-drained soil with a pH 6 to 8 but is adaptable to most soils as long as drainage is fast. It is slightly tolerant of saline soil and grows with 8 to 20 inches of precipitation.

Combine with bluebunch and western wheatgrass, buckwheat species, catclaw acacia, desert willow, gramagrasses, honey mesquite, juniper species, little sumac, mountain mahogany, piñon pine, prickly pear, and rabbit brush.

FLANNEL BUSH

Fremontodendron californicum
free-mon-toh-DEN-dron cal-ee-FOR-nic-um

- Bright yellow flowers in spring; olive green leaves
- Large evergreen shrub or small tree
- Foothills of mountains in California
- Zones 7 to 10

12'
12'

This broadleaf evergreen shrub or small tree grows 6 to 15 feet tall with densely hairy stems; thick, roundish, dull-green leaves; and brilliant clear yellow flowers up to 2½ inches in diameter. From spring to summer, it produces a mass of color, one flower opening at a time.

USE: Beautiful as specimen, in groups, a background for perennial garden, or espaliered. It is a most rewarding shrub in any garden setting.

CULTURE: Dry slopes of Sierra Nevada and coastal ranges of southern California mountains in chaparral, piñon-juniper open woodland, and ponderosa pine parkland communities are home to this shrub. It does best with low relative humidity, full to part sun, clay or loam, and well-drained, dryish soil, pH 6 to 8. Combine with buckwheat, chamise, greenleaf manzanita, and hairyleaf ceanothus.

Flannel bush leaves have tiny hairs, giving them a gray-green look.

NEW MEXICO PRIVET

Forestiera neomexicana
for-es-STEER-a ne-o-mex-i-CAN-a

- Bright green leaves, yellow flowers, dark blue fruit
- Large deciduous shrub or small tree
- Cold and warm deserts
- Zones 4 to 10

13'
10'

This upright, spreading, vase-shaped, large deciduous shrub or small tree, reaches 12 to 15 feet tall by 10 to 12 feet wide. Related to lilacs, forsythia, olive, and ash, its small, narrow, apple-green foliage presents an open-air texture for such a large plant. In spring, before leaves emerge, the plant bursts with small, fragrant yellow flowers. Soon blue-black, olivelike fruits develop that are favored by songbirds. Because male and female flowers are usually on different plants, both sexes are needed for fruit. Foliage is dense when moisture is available; however, leaves fall off under stress.

USE: Train as a small, multi-stem specimen tree, or shear it to make a formal hedge. Allow it to grow naturally as a windbreak, or encourage its natural suckering in order to develop a thicket as a barrier. Also a good container plant.

CULTURE: New Mexico privet is found on hillsides, mesas, and moist valleys with 10 to 20 inches of annual rainfall, in chaparral, open woodlands, deserts, and coastal sage scrub, at 3,000 to 7,000 feet in elevation. Drought and cold tolerant, it is adaptable to most soil. Regular deep watering accelerates growth, but overwatering results in borer problems. New Mexico privet develops a deep taproot and can be very drought tolerant once established. Provide good air circulation to avoid mildew.

Combine with California buckwheat, coyote brush, four-wing saltbush, gambel oak, purple sage, and squaw apple.

To survive extended droughts, New Mexico privet drops its leaves.

Fouquieria splendens
foo-KWEER-ree-uh SPLEN-dens

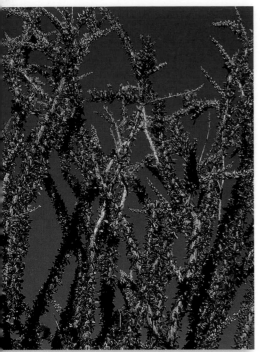

Orange-red ocotillo blooms appear reliably even in a dry spring.

OCOTILLO

- Tubular orange flowers in spring
- Vase-shaped, deciduous shrub
- Grasslands and chaparral of warm desert
- Zones 8 to 10

Ocotillo is a deciduous vase-shaped shrub with 6 to 100 upright branches arising from the crown. The spiny stems are 10 to 25 feet. Plant spread may be 15 feet. Thick, leathery leaves appear in the axil of the spine when moisture is available. They drop—and the plant enters dormancy—when under water stress. Ocotillo is mostly leafless. When leaves do appear, they are bright green and turn yellow to red in autumn. In spring, at the tips of these dramatic stems are panicles of tubular orange flowers, each one up to 1 foot long. The effect is unmistakable and dramatic.

USE: This is an outstanding accent plant in a texture or succulent garden. With careful placement, it can create interesting wall silhouettes. Use cut stems as a natural fence. The flowers attract hummingbirds.

CULTURE: Ocotillo is a plant of the warm desert and thrives in dry, well-drained, rocky slopes, mesas, plains, and valleys of desert shrub, desert grassland, chaparral, Texas savanna, and open woodland communities. The soils where they grow best are often underlain by caliche. Generally it is found between sea level and 5,200 feet elevation. Grow it in full sun and reflected heat. It tolerates salt, but plant in well-drained sites or on a slope. It does need good drainage. Once planted, support until established.

Combine with acacia, agave, cacti, creosote bush, and palo verde.

Leucophyllum frutescens
lew-ko-FY-lum fru-TES-ens

TEXAS SAGE

- Silver leaves and purple flowers
- Rounded evergreen shrub
- Chihuahuan desert
- Zones 8 to 10

This compact, rounded, silver evergreen shrub is 4 to 8 feet tall and 3 to 6 feet wide with outstanding ornamental features. Leaves are oval shaped and covered with soft, silver-blue, gray hairs. Flowers are lavender to purple, covering the entire plant in early summer and then sporadically throughout the year.

USE: A rugged, drought tolerant plant, it is excellent accented against dark needle evergreens. Use as a hedge or barrier (spaced 5 feet apart) or around foundations. Can be sheared, and grown in containers. Or use its spectacular silver foliage in a theme garden.

CULTURE: Texas sage grows naturally on the plains and plateaus of the Chihuahuan desert on alkaline, gravelly, or sandy soils. It thrives with less than 10 inches of rainfall a year. Plant in full sun as it tolerates reflected heat. Shade will open it up and reduce flowering. Grow in well-drained, neutral to alkaline soil. Do not fertilize. Water carefully until established. Use supplemental water sparingly to keep it blooming. Let it dry out between watering. It does not do well in humid environments.

Combine with various cacti, catclaw acacia, globe mallow, juniper, ocotillo, penstemon species, piñon pine, three-leaf sumac, juniper species, and Arizona fuschia.

Compact Texas sage (**Leucophyllum frutescens** 'Compactum') has pink flowers and is smaller than the species.

Mahonia trifoliata
(syn. *Berberis trifoliata*)
ma-HONE-ee-a try-FOL-ee-a-ta

- Clusters of yellow flowers in spring
- Upright, arching evergreen shrub
- Warm deserts
- Zones 6 to 10

6'

4'

Algerita is a dense, upright to arching evergreen shrub that grows from 3 to 10 feet tall and 3 to 7 feet wide. It often grows alone but also may grow in thickets. Leaves are pale green to blue, hollylike with three spiny leaflets. In early spring, the plant blooms with lemon yellow clusters of flowers on the upper ends of the branches. The contrast with the blue foliage is very restful. The round, lustrous red berries (eventually ripening to bluish-black) are acidic and aromatic.

USE: Algerita is a four-season plant. It is an excellent specimen, barrier, or background plant. It works well in a dryland garden that uses blue foliage plants.

CULTURE: Algerita grows naturally on warm deserts, on slopes and flats in chaparral, grassland, shrubland, open woodland, parkland, and savanna communities, from sea level to 6,000 feet in elevation. It needs full sun on a variety of soil types, including clay, loam, and gravelly soil, pH 6.5 to 8. Drainage is most critical. It can grow on less than 10 or more than 20 inches of water per year.

Combine with buffalograss, gramagrasses, honey mesquite, juniper species, lechuguilla, little walnut, littleleaf sumac, live oak species, netleaf hackberry, piñon pine, sotol, threeawn grass, and yucca species.

AGARITA, ALGERITA

RELATED SPECIES: *Mahonia fremontii*, the Fremont mahonia, is an evergreen shrub with blue, hollylike foliage, 3 to 14 feet tall, with yellow flowers and yellow to brown fruits. It grows in flats and slopes in warm and lower cold-desert grassland and piñon-juniper woodlands, 3700 to 7000 feet; Zone 5.

Mahonia haematocarpa, red mahonia, is an evergreen shrub that is 3 to 12 feet tall with grayish-green foliage, yellow flowers, and juicy red fruit. It grows on slopes and mesas in warm desert shrubland and grassland, and in dry oak woodland, from 2,700 to 7,500 feet in elevation, also in Zone 5.

Mahonia foliage and flowers are often used in floral arrangements because of their strong form and long-lasting qualities. Fruits are edible and used in making jams.

A prickly broadleaf evergreen, algerita creates an impenetrable barrier. Red berries appear in fall.

Red mahonia (*Mahonia haematocarpa*) has five to nine leaflets and is a larger shrub than algerita.

Shrubs *continued*

Mahonia repens
ma-HONE-ee-a REE-penz

Creeping hollygrape is a low-growing evergreen shrub with holly-like leaves.

CREEPING HOLLYGRAPE

- Yellow flowers in spring
- Low-growing evergreen shrub
- Western mountains and Great Basin desert
- Zones 4 to 10

Creeping hollygrape is a broadleaf, perennial evergreen shrub with low to prostrate growth form. Stems may be 4 to 18 inches tall depending on growing conditions. Each stem arises from an underground stem (rhizome). These allow the plant to spread and eventually cover large areas. Leaves are spine-tipped (like a holly), green in spring, and burgundy-tinted in fall and winter. In spring showy yellow flowers appear and are soon followed by bunches of blue berries that resemble grapes (hence the common name).

USE: This plant is an adaptable broadleaf evergreen. It makes an excellent groundcover under trees and shrubs or a good transition plant between foundation shrubbery and lawn. Hollygrape is useful as a lawn replacement, especially in narrow or shaded areas.

CULTURE: Hollygrape grows in many environments in various plant communities, including western mountains and the Great Basin. It adapts to various soil types in open woodland, parkland, and sagebrush communities, from sea level to 10,000 feet. It tolerates full sun in winter and moist to dry soil. It also grows in shade and tolerates clay to gravelly soil, pH 6 to 8. Water until established and then periodically once it attains the desired size.

Combine with big sagebrush, bur and gambel oak, juniper species, ninebark, ponderosa pine, Saskatoon serviceberry, snowberry, and wax currant.

Quercus turbinella
KWER-kus tur-bin-EL-a

- Olive green, leathery leaves
- Spreading evergreen shrub
- Warm and cold deserts, chaparral, woodlands
- Zones 5 to 8

SHRUB LIVE OAK, TURBINELLA OAK

This broadleaf evergreen shrub or small tree grows 3 to 8 feet tall and spreads by underground stems, forming a dense thicket. Leaves are dull green, leathery, and hollylike.

USE: Plant as hedge or barrier, or train as small tree. It provides winter color.

CULTURE: Shrub live oak is found in canyons and swales of warm and cold deserts in chaparral, desert shrub, and open woodland communities from 2,000 to 8,000 feet in elevation.

It grows in sandy to clay loam, pH 6.5 to 8, in deep or shallow soil. It is more tolerant of drought with deeper soil. Grow in sunny south or east exposure with 15 to 20 inches of precipitation.

Combine with blue gramagrass, broom snakeweed, desert ceanothus, mountain mahogany, piñon pine, pointleaf and pringle manzanita, single-seed juniper, sugar- and three-leaf sumac.

Shrub live oak is a chaparral plant with thick, gray-green, hollylike evergreen leaves.

THREE-LEAF SUMAC

Rhus trilobata
ROOS try-low-BAH-ta

- Yellow flowers in spring; prominent red leaves in fall
- Rounded, deciduous shrub
- Common throughout western North America
- Zones 3 to 8

Three-leaf sumac is a rounded, deciduous shrub that reaches 3 to 6 feet tall and wide. Leaves are bright green and prominently red in fall. Yellow flowers come in dense clusters at branch tips and are followed by red, berrylike fruits. It is a very clean and attractive plant throughout the year.

USE: It is excellent cover for slopes and makes a good foundation plant in informal, formal, or naturalized gardens.

CULTURE: Three-leaf sumac grows across western North America, from warm to cold deserts, to the western Great Plains. It's found growing on hillsides, in canyons, and along waterways in open woodlands, desert and sage scrub, and parkland communities, at elevations from 3,500 to 11,000 feet. Three-leaf sumac tolerates dry to moist, alkaline to acid soil (pH 6.5 to 8.5), and sun to partial shade. The plant's salt tolerance is fair.

Combine with Apache plume, cliff rose, chokecherry, creeping hollygrape, gambel oak, juniper species, mountain mahogany, pine species, and shrub live oak.

RELATED SPECIES: *Rhus microphylla*, littleleaf desert sumac, is a small to medium shrub from desert foothills, open woodlands, and Texas savanna. Compared to three-leaf sumac, everything other than its size is miniature (foliage, flowers and fruit).

Fruits can make a lemonade-like drink.

Rhus microphylla **is noted for its very small leaves.**

NEW MEXICO LOCUST

Robinia neomexicana
rob-BIN-ee-ah ne-o-mex-i-KAHN-a

- Pink flowers in late spring
- Upright, deciduous shrub
- Warm and cold deserts, woodlands, parklands, grasslands
- Zones 4 to 8

New Mexico locust is a spiny, deciduous shrub or small, upright, rounded tree. It ranges in height from 12 to 15 feet and spreads by underground stems (rhizomes), forming large thickets with dark grayish-green leaves. The showy, pink to rose flowers come in 2- to 4-inch-long hanging clusters in late spring to early summer. Fruits are interesting pea pods because of their hairy bristles.

USE: Valued for its flowers and ability to form an impenetrable thicket, windbreak, or hedge, it is good for erosion control on slopes and along waterways.

CULTURE: New Mexico locust grows in warm and cold deserts along waterways, canyons, and slopes in open woodlands, parklands, and grasslands, at elevations from 4,000 to 8,500 feet. It is adaptable to many soil types and prefers pH 6 to 8.5. It thrives with as little as 12 inches of precipitation per year; less water means a shorter plant. Full sun is preferred, but partial shade is fine (though flowering is diminished). Since roots naturally extract nitrogen from the air, the plant needs little fertilizer. The plant is difficult to move once established.

Combine with Arizona fescue, fendler ceanothus, manzanita species, snowberry, mountain mahogany, mutton bluegrass, and western yarrow.

New Mexico locust has branches with pink blooms and small spines at the base of grayish-green leaves.

Perennials

Achillea lanulosa
(syn. *Achillea millefolium lanulosa*)
a-ki-LEE-a lan-you-LOW-sa

Yarrow flowers are excellent for fresh and dry floral arrangements.

WESTERN YARROW

- White flowers
- Herbaceous perennial
- Throughout North America, especially western deserts and woodlands
- Zones 2 to 8

Western yarrow is an herbaceous perennial that grows 6 to 18 inches tall. Foliage is mostly basal with few to many erect stems. The gray-green leaves have a very dissected, ferny appearance. Flowers are small, white, sometimes pink and come in clusters on erect stems. Numerous variations of this species exist, and it may be evergreen depending on conditions.

USE: Western yarrow can be used in rock gardens, perennial borders, cutting gardens, or in naturalized prairie gardens. It spreads by short underground stems, colonizing small areas. Useful as ground cover, it tolerates some foot traffic but needs mowing. Use fresh or dried flowers in floral arrangements.

CULTURE: Western yarrow grows in a variety of soil types and habitats across North America, including warm and cold deserts, the Great Plains, open woodlands, forests, savanna, and chaparral, at elevations from 2,400 to 11,000 feet. Plant it in full sun or partial shade in any soil type, preferably with a pH 6 to 8. It will grow with less than 12 inches of precipitation.

Combine with Arkansas rose, big sagebrush, bluebunch and western wheatgrass, buckwheat species, gambel oak, June grass, Idaho fescue, juniper, needle grass, penstemon species, and wax currant.

RELATED SPECIES: *Artemisia millefolium*, common yarrow, is a very similar European species often mistaken for a native. It is available in flower colors of pink to red.

Antennaria parvifolia
an-te-NA-ri-a par-va-FOL-ee-a

LITTLELEAF PUSSY-TOES

- White flowers; silvery leaves
- Low and spreading
- Warm and cold deserts, chaparral, and woodlands
- Zones 3 to 8

Littleleaf pussy-toes is a mat-forming evergreen perennial, 1½ to 6 inches high, spreading by short prostrate stems, 1 to 6 inches long. Leaves are very small (less than ½ inch), mostly at ground level and covered with silvery hairs. White sometimes pink, clustered, disk flowers on 8-inch stems rise above the foliage. Flowers resemble cat's toes (hence the common name).

Antennaria dioica is similar to littleleaf pussy-toes. The common name comes from clusters of soft, furry flower heads.

USE: It is excellent around edges of walks, between flagstones, or around rocks in prairie or silver gardens.

CULTURE: Littleleaf pussy-toes grows naturally on the plains and gentle slopes of western mountains, in warm and cold deserts, as well as on the Great Plains, in sage and chaparral shrubland, piñon-juniper woodland, and prairie grassland communities. Plants grow well in loam to clay soil at elevations from 5,000 to 10,000 feet. It will grow in full sun in cool, moist areas or light, dry shade in warmer sites. It grows with as little as 12 to 15 inches of rain annually. Combine with bluebunch and western wheatgrass, buckwheat species, cutleaf fleabane, lupine, phlox, prairie June grass, sumac, and western yarrow.

RELATED SPECIES: *Antennaria rosea*, pussy-toes, has white to pink flowers.

Artemisia frigida

are-tah-MEES-ee-a FRIJ-i-duh

- Small yellow flowers in spring; silver-gray leaves
- Low shrub or herbaceous perennial
- Widely distributed throughout western North America
- Zones 3 to 8

16"
12"

Fringed sage is a soft-stemmed, herbaceous perennial shrub, but in many situations the stems become woody near the plant's base more like a sub-shrub. It grows 8 to 18 inches tall and about 12 inches wide. Its short, leafy stems produce a matlike cover. Leaves are finely cut, soft, silver-gray and evergreen. Yellow disk flowers are small and borne in profusion on slightly nodding stems. **USE:** Useful in dryland perennial borders, in prairie meadows, or in

FRINGED SAGE

foliage, texture, or silver gardens. It is a good dryland substitute for *Artemisia* 'Silver Mound'.

CULTURE: Fringed sage is found throughout western North America from Canada to Mexico, at elevations from 3,000 to 11,000 feet, in the Great Plains, warm and cold deserts, open woodlands, parklands, and savannas. The plant is widely adapted, growing well in full sun or partial shade in most soils, preferring a normal pH 6 to 8.5. It grows well with 8 to 12 inches of annual rain. Extra watering promotes more rapid growth but may cause crown rot. Remove flower stems midsummer to keep plant's neat appearance.

Combine with blue flax, blackfoot daisy, desert zinnia, dotted gay feather, Indian paintbrush, penstemon species, scarlet globe mallow, and western yarrow. **RELATED SPECIES:** *Artemisia ludoviciana*, white sage, has silver

foliage and an open, loose form. It spreads by underground stems and naturalizes in prairie gardens. Varieties are available for silver foliage and more bush form.

Fringed sage gets its name from the small divided leaves that give the appearance of fringed threads.

Asclepias tuberosa

as-KLEE-pee-us too-beh-ROW-suh

- Bright orange, red, or yellow flowers in summer
- Herbaceous perennial
- Great Plains prairies
- Zones 3 to 8

2'
1'

Butterfly weed is an upright perennial with rough, hairy, narrow green leaves, and bright orange (rarely red or yellow) flowers in summer. Unlike other milkweeds, it does not have milky sap. The flowers produce large amounts of nectar to attract various adult butterflies as well as the monarch caterpillars. They store the toxic substance from the plant to ward off predators. **USE:** Plant in perennial, cutting, or butterfly garden. Use dried fruits in floral arrangements.

BUTTERFLY WEED

CULTURE: Butterfly weed grows naturally in dry, open soil throughout the Great Plains prairie, from sea level to 7,000 feet in elevation. It is a variable species with a wide range of tolerance to drought, soil, and heat. Grow it in well-drained, moist to dry soil in full sun. It may take two years to establish, as roots develop first, and does not transplant once established. Remove spent blooms to encourage second bloom. Keep moist in flower, but do not overwater. It is slow to emerge in spring and dies back to the ground in winter.

Combine with aster, black-eyed Susan, blue gramagrass, little bluestem, prairie June grass, three-leaf sumac, silver lead plant, and western wheatgrass.

Bright orange flowers of butterfly weed produce nectar that is attractive to butterflies.

Perennials *continued*

DESERT MARIGOLD

Baileya multiradiata
BAY-lee-uh mul-tee-RAD-ee-a-ta

- Bright yellow flowers
- Short-lived perennial
- Warm deserts
- Zones 7 to 10

Desert marigold is a short-lived perennial that grows 12 to 14 inches tall and wide. Its broad, oval leaves are silvery gray-green, with golden-yellow flowers 2 inches in diameter. They bloom from spring until frost.

USE: Use in a dryland perennial border or in mass plantings, container, and butterfly gardens. It self-sows in sandy soil.

CULTURE: Desert marigold grows naturally in warm deserts in sandy to gravelly soil; also in desert scrub and desert grassland, open woodlands, and chaparral communities. Plant it in full sun with minimal water in a well-drained site with pH 7 to 9. Do not use any organic mulch near it.

Combine with agave, cholla, cliff rose, fernbush, globe mallow, mimosa, ocotillo, prickly pear, and sumac.

Desert marigold blooms almost continuously, from frost to frost.

CHOCOLATE FLOWER

Berlandiera lyrata
ber-lan-dee-AIR-uh lye-RAY-tuh

- Pale yellow flowers spring through summer
- Herbaceous perennial
- Warm and cold deserts
- Zones 4 to 8

Chocolate flower is an herbaceous perennial with upright stems, 12 to 15 inches tall, that droop as they mature. The leaves are pale green and mostly at the base. Light yellow, chocolate-scented, daisylike flowers bloom spring through summer. The ray flowers are light yellow surrounding an orange disk center. Beneath the flower heads are green cup-shaped bracts that remain once the petals drop.

This looks like a green eye daisy, an additional common name for this flower. The cup holds the chocolate-colored seeds when they ripen. Chocolate flowers attract butterflies.

USE: Use this reliable plant in prairie or naturalized gardens (reseeds in sandy soil). The fruit is used in floral arrangements.

CULTURE: It is found in warm and cold deserts, in sunny shrub and grassland communities, and along roadsides and basins where water runoff collects, from 4,000 to 7,000 feet in elevation. Place in full sun in sandy or gravelly soil with minimal organic matter. It grows with less than 12 inches of water. Flowers may droop in midday sun. Transplant before deep roots develop, or it is difficult to move.

Combine with blackfoot daisy, blue flax, phlox penstemon, fern verbena, fringed sage, gramagrasses, and winecup.

Chocolate flower has a mild chocolate scent.

TRAILING INDIGO BUSH

Dalea greggii
DAY-lee-uh GREG-ee-i

- Lavender to purple flowers
- Herbaceous perennial; low shrub
- Warm deserts
- Zones 8 to 9

18"
18"

Trailing indigo bush is a low, mounding shrub 1 to 2 feet high and wide, with trailing stems. The silvery-gray leaves are silky, fine textured, and usually persistent. Lavender to purple flowers come throughout spring and summer.

USE: This plant is a good small area groundcover, used massed on slopes for erosion control or trailing over the edges of containers and hanging baskets. It does not respond well to mowing or shearing; cut it back only to prevent its becoming too woody.

CULTURE: It thrives throughout warm desert shrublands in rocky, limestone soil. Plant in full sun to light shade in well-drained sites; it is very drought tolerant once established. The roots are able to absorb atmospheric nitrogen.

Trailing indigo bush is a fast-growing plant for soil stabilization.

PURPLE PRAIRIE CLOVER

Dalea purpurea
(syn. Petalostemon purpureum)
DAY-lee-uh purr-PURR-ee-uh

- Purple flowers
- Herbaceous perennial
- Great Plains grasslands
- Zones 4 to 9

18"
9'

Purple prairie clover is a soft-stemmed, open, vase-shaped perennial. It grows 15 to 25 inches tall; leaves are divided into five narrow, shiny green segments that produce a fine-textured appearance. Numerous 1- to 3-inch-long purple flowers come in dense spikes in late spring and summer.

USE: Best in meadow gardens, its deep taproot is also valuable in erosion control or on steep slopes.

CULTURE: Purple prairie clover grows throughout the Great Plains grasslands in various soil types on mesas, hillsides, plains, and partially shaded ravines. It grows well in a variety of soils, moist to very dry, and tolerates pH 6 to 8.5. It survives on as little as 15 inches of rainfall a year. Roots are able to fix atmospheric nitrogen, minimizing fertilizer needs.

Combine with Arkansas rose, black-eyed Susan, blue gramagrass, buffalograss, western wheatgrass, dotted gay feather, phlox penstemon, silver lead plant, and yellow sundrop.

Flowers of purple prairie clover open first at the base of the flower and gradually move upwards.

INCIENSO

Encelia farinosa
en-SEE-lee-uh far-ih-NOH-sa

- Yellow flowers in spring
- Rounded shrub
- Warm and cold deserts
- Zones 8 to 10

4'
4'

Incienso is a low-growing perennial shrub that grows 3 to 5 feet tall and wide. Growth is fast, but the plant is relatively short-lived. Its leaves are gray-green and clustered mostly at branch ends. Leaves drop when the plant is water stressed. Vibrant yellow flowers come in spring.

USE: Incienso is a good choice for mass plantings along foundations, naturalized with desert plants, or in containers for spring color.

CULTURE: It grows naturally throughout warm and cold deserts on flats, slopes, and mesas in chaparral, sagebrush, open woodland and desert grassland communities, at elevations up to 3,000 feet. It prefers dry, gravelly, slightly alkaline soil, though it takes proximity to heat-reflecting desert pavement in stride.

Vibrant yellow flowers of incienso open in late winter and spring.

Epilobium canum canum
(syn. Zauschneria californica)
ep-ih-LOW-bee-um CAN-um CAN-um

Orange-red, trumpet-shaped flowers of *Epilobium canum* attract hummingbirds.

CALIFORNIA FUCHSIA, HUMMINGBIRD TRUMPET

- Bright red flowers
- Perennial
- Deserts and dry slopes
- Zones 7 to 10

California fuchsia is a perennial that grows 1½ to 2 feet tall by 2 to 3 feet wide. It is upright, arching, and mounded in form, with rigid, brittle stems. Leaves are narrow, grayish-green, and covered with soft hairs. Bright red tubular flowers are showy in summer and very attractive to hummingbirds.

USE: California fuchsia is a good choice for informal plantings, wildlife gardens, dryland perennial and mixed borders, or container gardens. Its short, spreading underground stems are effective on slopes, especially combined with sagebrush and other chaparral plants.

CULTURE: California fuchsia grows in deserts and dry slopes and ridges in chaparral, coastal sage scrub, and pine woodlands, from sea level to 10,000 feet in elevation. Plants prefer well-drained, sandy to loam soil, and full sun; they grow poorly in clay soil. Trim in winter or early spring to control plant shape and size. It requires less than 12 inches of rain or irrigation per year.

Combine with agave, dudleya, evening primrose, manzanita, mountain mahogany, penstemon, sagebrush, and yucca.

RELATED SPECIES: *Epilobium canum latifolium*, Arizona fuchsia, is a shrubby perennial; Zones 5 to 9. *Epilobium canum garrettii* 'Orange Carpet' (syn. *Zauschneria garrettii*) is hardy to 8,000 feet and Zones 3 to 8. It is compact with light green, narrow leaves and orange flowers.

Erigeron compositus
ee-RIJ-er-on kom-POZ-ee-tus

Finely-divided, fuzzy, gray-green leaves give cutleaf fleabane a soft, delicate texture.

CUTLEAF FLEABANE

- White, pink, or blue flowers
- Low-growing perennial
- Great Plains grasslands
- Zones 4 to 7

Cutleaf fleabane is a low-growing perennial that reaches 3 to 10 inches tall and 6 to 12 inches wide. It is a refined plant with white (sometimes pink to bluish) daisy flowers and delicate, cutleaf, woolly, silver-gray dissected leaves. Blooms appear midspring to summer.

USE: This plant is an excellent choice for edging in dryland perennial gardens, for naturalized prairie landscapes, and for rock gardens, or crevices of stone walls.

CULTURE: Cutleaf fleabane grows naturally on rocky, gravelly, and sandy soils on mesas and hills in parkland and grassland communities of the Great Plains, at elevations of 5,000 feet or more. It prefers sun to partial shade in well-drained soils that are slightly alkaline, pH 7 to 8. It is more vigorous in sandy loam than in clay. Cutleaf fleabane combines well with many silver-gray plants.

Combine with blue gramagrass, buffalograss, foothills penstemon, fringed sage, Indian paintbrush, prairie June grass, sundrops, three-leaf sumac, and wax currant.

RELATED SPECIES: *Erigeron caespitosus*, tufted fleabane, has white, blue to pink flowers and similar silver-gray foliage.

Eriogonum fasciculatum foliosum
e-ri-OG-o-num fas-sik-yoo-LAH-tum
fo-lee-OH-sum

- ■ Pink to white flowers
- ■ Flowering perennial
- ■ Warm and cold deserts
- ■ Zones 7 to 10

30"

30"

California buckwheat is a long-lived woody perennial that grows 1 to 3 feet tall and wide. Bundled (fascicled) leaves are narrow, gray-green above and silvery beneath. Pinkish to white flowers come on terminal clusters and persist for a long bloom period.

USE: California buckwheat is a good addition to dry-garden perennial borders, as well as rock, bee, and butterfly gardens. This subspecies is more drought tolerant and more floriferous than *Eriogonum fasiculatum*.

CULTURE: Plants thrive in warm and cold deserts, on dry slopes and

CALIFORNIA BUCKWHEAT

canyons, in desert scrub, open woodlands, and chaparral communities, at elevations from 1,000 to 4,500 feet. Plants require full sun and become gangly in too much shade. Sandy to clay soil is preferred, pH 6 to 8. Annual rain (or irrigation) of only 8 to 12 inches is required. Cut back to renew growth from the base.

Combine with big sagebrush, ceanothus, ephedra, Joshua tree, juniper, live shrub oak, manzanita, mountain mahogany, piñon pine, and western redbud.

California buckwheat blooms at times and in locations that few other flowers do, making it highly desirable to bees and other pollen-consuming insects.

Eriogonum umbellatum
e-ri-OG-o-num um-bel-LAH-tum

- ■ Sulfur yellow flowers
- ■ Perennial
- ■ Mountains, cold deserts, Great Plains
- ■ Zones 3 to 8

8"

10"

Sulfur flower is a low-growing perennial that grows 6 to 12 inches high by 8 to 12 inches wide or larger. Notable for being attractive in all seasons, clusters of yellow flowers rise above basal foliage on 6 to 8 inch stalks in spring. Flowers last several weeks, eventually changing to shades of orange and red. Foliage is dark green above, white with hairs underneath, turning red to brown in fall.

USE: Place in rock gardens, between crevices, or as a border or edging plant or groundcover for small areas. Pick flowers before maturity to retain

SULFUR FLOWER

brilliant color. They are effective in dried floral arrangements if stems are long enough.

CULTURE: Sulfur flower grows in mountainous areas, cold desert shrublands, Great Plains grasslands, open woodlands on rocky outcrops, dry valleys, and mesas, at elevations of 4,000 feet or more. Plant in sun or light shade, gravelly or well-drained soil, pH 5 to 7.5. Supplemental irrigation increases growth, flowers, and foliage. It is very cold tolerant. Combine with blue gramagrass, cutleaf fleabane, foothills penstemon, fringed sage, globe mallow, hummingbird trumpet, greenleaf manzanita, little bluestem, phlox, prairie June grass, western wheatgrass, and western yarrow.

RECOMMENDED VARIETIES AND RELATED SPECIES: *Eriogonum umbellatum* 'Shasta Sulfur' buckwheat has larger flowers, is more robust than the species, but is less hardy, to Zone 5. *E. jamesii*, James wild buckwheat, has white flowers and grows on dry rocky slopes and shale soils of the Great Plains and deserts; Zones 4 to 8.

Eriogonum umbellatum polyanthum 'Shasta Sulfur' is a mounding plant with yellow flowers that age to orange.

Perennials *continued*

Gaillardia pinnatifida
gay-LAR-di-a pin-nat-ih-FY-duh

SLENDER BLANKET FLOWER

- **Yellow flowers with red centers**
- **Perennial**
- **Warm and cold deserts; arid Great Plains**
- **Zones 5 to 8**

Blanket flower is a perennial that grows slightly less than 2 feet tall. Its delicate, gray-green leaves are finely divided and mostly present on the lower half of the stem. Daisylike flowers with red centers bloom all summer.

USE: Use blanket flower to naturalize in meadow gardens, and combine with ornamental grasses. It makes a delicate, light-textured accent among coarser perennials and foliage plants.

CULTURE: This plant naturally grows throughout warm and cold deserts

Slender blanket flower has finer texture than other gaillardias.

and arid Great Plains, in dry fields and along roadsides, usually at elevations below 6,800 feet.

Combine it with Apache plume, aster species, blue gramagrass, cliff rose, Indian paintbrush, singleleaf ash, tansy aster, blackfoot daisy, penstemon species, threeawn grass, and western yarrow.

RELATED SPECIES: *Gaillardia aristata*, blanket flower, is a more common, coarser species, that blooms the first year from seed. It has yellow and bronze-red flowers and dark green, elongated foliage. 'Dazzler' has yellow and maroon flowers on 2 to 3 foot perennial plants, and is also easy to grow from seed; hardy to Zone 2. 'Yellow Queen' is a large plant with yellow flowers with gold centers. It blooms summer until frost, and is very heat and drought tolerant; hardy to Zone 2.

Gutierrezia sarothrae
(syn. Xanthocephalum sarothrae)
goo-tee-er-REZ-ee-uh sa-ROW-thray

BROOM SNAKEWEED

- **Yellow flowers**
- **Perennial**
- **Warm and cold deserts; Great Plains to woodlands**
- **Zones 4 to 8**

This upright, rounded, shrubby, herbaceous perennial is 8 to 15 inches tall by 6 to 20 inches wide. Brittle stems fan out like a broom for interesting winter form. Stems rise from a single taproot. Foliage is small, fine-textured, and bright green, with a sandpapery surface. Small yellow flowers are numerous in late summer and early fall.

Snakeweed develops two types of roots. The taproot allows it to access water deep in the soil. Lateral roots

Broom snakeweed blooms late summer to fall.

produce a cork-like protection to prevent moisture loss under dry conditions. Under moist conditions, the cork coating breaks down.

USE: Plant in rock gardens, prairie or cutting gardens, or in containers.

CULTURE: Broom snakeweed is widely distributed from warm and cold deserts to the Great Plains, in grassland, shrubland, and open woodland communities. It grows on rocky plains, dry foothills, ridgetops, mountain slopes, and semi-desert valleys, from 3,000 to 7,000 feet in elevation. Plant it in a sunny site with a deep, well-drained soil, from gravel to heavy clay, pH 6.5 to 8. It grows quickly with available water, goes dormant, and drops leaves under water stress.

Combine with aster, desert zinnia, dotted gayfeather, ephedra, globe mallow, gramagrasses, honey mesquite, and winterfat.

Ipomoea leptophylla
ip-oh-MEE-uh lep-toh-FYE-luh

- Magenta flowers
- Perennial
- Sand prairie grasslands of the Great Plains
- Zones 4 to 8

3'
4'

Bush morning glory is a bushy perennial that grows 2 to 4 feet tall and wide. Its leaves are shiny green, willowlike, and about 5 inches long. The large, magenta, funnel-shaped flowers appear throughout summer. Plants grow from large underground storage stems up to 4 feet long. Leaves and stems emerge in late spring and then die back in winter.

USE: This is an excellent addition to dryland perennial gardens and naturalistic plantings among mixed-grass or sand prairie landscapes.

BUSH MORNING GLORY

CULTURE: Grow bush morning glory in a sunny place, in well-drained loam to sandy soil. It is very drought tolerant and needs minimal care.

Combine it with native asters, broom snakeweed, gayfeather, prairie baby's breath, buckwheat, evening star, needle-and-thread grass, rabbit brush, and silver buffaloberry.

Bush morning glory is a very long-lived, drought-tolerant perennial.

Melampodium leucanthum
mel-am-POH-dee-um. lew-KAN-thum

- White flowers with yellow centers
- Perennial
- Warm and cold deserts
- Zones 5 to 9

8"
12"

This herbaceous perennial (sometimes annual), low-mounded plant is 6 to 12 inches tall and up to 16 inches wide. It has soft, gray, small, narrow foliage and 1-inch, yellow-centered white daisies that bloom spring through summer or winter in warm climates.

USE: This is a dryland perennial or rock garden plant that thrives in beds as a low border plant or naturalized in a prairie landscape; it combines well with cacti and other succulents.

CULTURE: Blackfoot daisy grows naturally on rocky outcrops and dry

BLACKFOOT DAISY

limestone soils in warm and cold desert shrublands and Great Plains short-grass prairie. Plant it in average to lean, well-drained soils, in full sun. It tolerates reflected heat, but not moist or wet soil. It is short-lived, has brittle stems, and does not tolerate foot (or paw) traffic.

Combine it with buffalograss, blue gramagrass, desert zinnia, phlox penstemon, purple groundcherry, sand cherry, scarlet globe mallow, sundrops, and verbena species.

Blackfoot daisy blooms from spring to fall.

Perennials *continued*

Mimulus longiflorus
(syn. *Diplacus longiflorus*)
MIM-you-lus long-ih-FLO-russ

- White, pink or yellow flowers
- Perennial
- Coastal sage and chaparral
- Zones 9 to 10

SOUTHERN BUSH MONKEY FLOWER

30"
36"

Southern bush monkey flower is a perennial that grows 2 to 3 feet tall by 2 to 4 feet wide. Its form is mounded with narrow, long, green leaves and sticky stems. It thins out or sheds leaves under drought stress. Many yellow, white or pink, 2-inch-long, funnel-shaped flowers cover the plant in late summer.

USE: Use southern bush monkey flower in perennial borders and as a container plant.

CULTURE: The plant grows naturally on steep slopes, in dry foothills and plains, as well as disturbed sites in coarse soils among coastal sage scrub and chaparral communities.

Plant it in full sun in well-drained soil. Once established, it requires little or no supplemental irrigation. To keep tidy, remove water-stressed stems and foliage.

Combine with California buckeye, ceanothus, hummingbird trumpet vine, large-flowered penstemon, manzanita, salvia, and western redbud.

Two-inch velvety flowers of *Mimulus longiflorus* are attractive to hummingbirds.

Mirabilis multiflora
mih-RAB-ih-liss mul-ti-FLOR-ah

GIANT FOUR O'CLOCK, DESERT FOUR O'CLOCK

- Magenta flowers
- Perennial
- Warm and cold deserts
- Zones 4 to 8

18"
30"

Giant four-o'clock is a perennial that grows 1 to 2 feet tall and 2 to 3 feet wide. Its blue-green leaves are thick, downy, and rounded to heart-shaped. Numerous magenta, trumpet-shaped flowers open at dusk and close again at dawn. It sprouts in spring from an underground root (tuber), then dies back with the first frost, leaving an open space at the soil surface.

USE: This plant is attractive cascading over walls or growing between large boulders. Plant along dry streambeds or at base of needled evergreens, but consider how to fill the void they leave during the dormant season.

CULTURE: Giant four-o'clock grows in both warm and cold deserts where soil is favorable, in open ground, in rock crevices, on hillsides, or among shrubland, piñon-juniper, and oak woodlands. It generally grows at elevations from 2,300 to 7,500 feet. Grow it in full sun in well-drained soil; avoid placing it in locations of either heavy clay or poor drainage.

Combine with agave, cacti, cliff rose, desert mountain mahogany, ephedra, juniper, manzanita, piñon pine, and yucca.

RELATED SPECIES: *Mirabilis jalapa*, four-o'clock, is a more common, old-fashioned annual plant from warm deserts. Its flowers are pink, white, yellow, red, orange, lavender or mixed colors.

Magenta flowers earn the plant's name "mirabilis," which is Latin for marvelous.

Oenothera caespitosa
ee-noh-THEE-rah kess-pi-TOH-suh

- White flowers
- Perennial
- Warm and cold deserts; Great Plains
- Zones 4 to 8

10"

18"

This perennial is a mounded plant with elongated, velvety green leaves. It forms dense rosettes 6 to 12 inches high and 12 to 24 inches across. There are no visible above-ground stems. Flowers are 2 to 4 inches wide, white (aging to pink), and cuplike; they lay above tufted foliage and open in the afternoon and close the following morning.

USE: White tufted evening primrose is an excellent garden plant for borders, edging, dryland perennial beds, or simply naturalized in prairie gardens.

WHITE TUFTED EVENING PRIMROSE

CULTURE: The plant grows naturally in warm deserts and the Great Plains in shrub, grass, and woodland communities on sunny slopes and plains. It prefers clay to sandy soil, in elevations below 7,500 feet. Grow it in full sun or partial shade in well-drained, gritty soil with no organic amendment. It needs less than 8 inches of rain or irrigation a year to survive, but additional water increases bloom. Do not water in cool weather; it promotes rot. It is difficult to transplant once established because of the extensive fleshy root system.

Combine with cliff rose, curlleaf mountain mahogany, ephedra, fern verbena, globe mallow, juniper, paperflower, penstemon species, piñon pine, prickly pear, and yucca.

RELATED SPECIES: *Oenothera macrocarpa*, Ozark sundrop, has large lemon yellow flowers, and glossy green foliage.

The large white flowers of white tufted evening primrose open, age to pink, and die within one day.

Penstemon ambiguus
PEN-ste-mon am-BIG-you-us

- Pink to white flowers
- Perennial
- Warm deserts to Great Plains
- Zones 5 to 10

24"

24"

Phlox penstemon is a compact, airy perennial that grows up to 2 feet tall and wide. Its foliage is grasslike and dense on wiry stems. Pink to white flowers are similar to phlox. Overall the look is of a fine-textured, delicate plant.

USE: Grow in prairie gardens or in large groups in a dryland perennial border. It provides a billowy effect, or use it as an accent with fine-textured ornamental grasses.

CULTURE: Phlox penstemon grows in warm deserts, and the Great Plains, in desert shrublands, arroyos, and sandy grasslands. Plant in a well-drained site in full sun, in lean soil

PHLOX PENSTEMON

not amended with organic matter. This plant is sensitive to moist or wet soil when dormant and not tolerant of moisture around the crown. Do not use organic mulch. Combine with Apache plume, blackfoot daisy, blue flax, chocolate flower, cliff rose, desert zinnia, globe mallow, Mexican hat coneflower, sedum species, and spotted gayfeather.

Because of its fine texture, phlox penstemon is well-suited to short- and mixed-grass prairie gardens.

Penstemon grandiflorus
PEN-ste-mon gran-dih-FLOR-us

This is one of the largest penstemon flowers and is a hummingbird favorite.

LARGE FLOWERED PENSTEMON

- Lavender flowers
- Perennial
- Grasslands of the Great Plains
- Zones 4 to 8

Large flowered penstemon is a 2 to 4 foot tall perennial. Its large leaves are smooth, bluish-green, and characteristically clasped around the thick and sturdy stems. Fragrant, large lavender flowers appear in early summer and attract hummingbirds.

USE: This is an excellent accent plant in a dryland perennial border or cutting garden. It is also dramatic enough to stand on its own as a specimen plant.

CULTURE: Large flowered penstemon grows naturally in the prairie grasslands of the Great Plains. It prefers coarse, rocky to sandy soil, and full sun. It will not live in clay soil or soils amended with organic material. Drought tolerance is excellent, needing less than 12 inches of rain or irrigation a year. Once established, it may not need any water. Combine it with blanket flower and bush morning glory.

Penstemon pinifolius
PEN-ste-mon pin-ih-FOE-lee-us

Pineleaf penstemon makes an excellent groundcover or low border.

PINELEAF PENSTEMON

- Scarlet flowers; reddish-purple foliage in fall
- Perennial
- Warm deserts
- Zones 4 to 9

Pineleaf penstemon is an upright perennial (or low-growing shrub) that reaches 6 to 18 inches tall and wide. Its leaves are bright green, very fine, and needlelike. They change to reddish-purple in fall. Narrow, tubular, scarlet flowers last for several weeks. The plant spreads by short underground stems.

USE: Pineleaf penstemon is a good addition to most any perennial border or rock garden in arid environments. It is an excellent low border plant, small hedge, or groundcover.

CULTURE: This plant grows naturally in warm deserts on rocky soil in desert scrub and grassland communities. Plant it on sunny sites in well-drained, lean or enriched soil. It adapts to both very dry and moderately dry soils. Combine it with fringed sage, blue grama, piñon pine, sand cherry, and sundrops.

Psilostrophe tagetina
SILL-o-strof ta-ge-TEEN-a

Cooper's woolly paper flower

WOOLLY PAPER FLOWER

- Yellow flowers
- Perennial
- Warm deserts
- Zones 8 to 10

Woolly paper flower is a perennial that grows 1½ to 2 feet tall and wide. It has upright, woolly stems and a dense, rounded form. Leaves are narrow and nearly 4 inches long. Yellow flowers are profuse and long lasting. As they mature, they become papery (hence the common name).

USE: This is a low border perennial for dryland or prairie gardens. It grows well with cacti and succulents.

CULTURE: It grows naturally in warm deserts and in various soil types, on plains and mesas, in desert scrub, grasslands, and open woodland communities, at elevations from 4,000 to 7,000 feet. Plant in full sun in well-drained soil. Remove spent blooms to keep in bloom, and water periodically in summer. Shear in fall to encourage bushy growth.

Combine with asters, globe mallow, and penstemon.

PRAIRIE CONEFLOWER, MEXICAN HAT

Ratibida columnifera
ruh-TIB-ih-duh col-um-NIF-er-a

- Yellow to dark red flowers
- Short-lived perennial
- Short-grass prairie of the Great Plains
- Zones 4 to 10

18"

18"

Prairie coneflower is a perennial with one to several upright stems that reach 1 to 2 feet tall. Its grayish-green leaves are deeply divided, lending the plant a fine texture. Flowers consist of several hundred purplish-brown disk flowers along a cylindrical head, surrounded by bright yellow to dark red ray flowers surrounding the base.

USE: Grow in a naturalized setting where plants can reseed themselves.

CULTURE: Prairie coneflower grows naturally in sandy to clay soils, in mixed- and short-grass prairies of the Great Plains. Plant it in full sun in well-drained soil, where it tolerates a variety of soil types with pH 6.5 to 8.5.

Combine with blue flax, blue gramagrass, plains coreopsis, phlox penstemon, rabbit brush, scarlet gaura, threadleaf gaura, threadleaf groundsel, and western wheatgrass.

Mexican hat has an open, airy, delicate growth form. It is easy to naturalize in gardens.

BLACK-EYED SUSAN

Rudbeckia hirta
rood-BEK-ee-uh HER-ta

- Yellow flowers with brown centers
- Short-lived perennial
- Widely distributed, especially in Great Plains prairies
- Zones 3 to 10

18"

24"

Black-eyed Susan is a short-lived perennial that is often grown as an annual or biennial. Its height is 1 to 2 feet or more. The lower leaves are rough-textured and diamond-shaped; leaves are higher up with lance-shaped stems. Flower heads are yellow with purplish-brown centers. The bloom period is long, from early summer into fall. Numerous selections are available, some grown as annuals and a few with much larger flowers.

USE: This perennial serves well in many capacities, including borders, cutting gardens, and naturalized prairie gardens.

CULTURE: Black-eyed Susan grows in various soil types throughout most of North America but is most abundant in the Great Plains prairies, piñon-juniper open woodlands, sandhills, and roadsides. Grow in clay to sandy loam soils, in full sun to partial shade. Water needs are low to moderate. Remove spent flowers to keep in bloom.

Combine with blue gramagrass, gambel oak, gayfeather, juniper, little bluestem, penstemon species, piñon, silver lead plant, snowberry, smooth, sumac, sunflower species, and three-leaf sumac.

Rudbeckia 'Indian Summer' is noted for its late summer flowers and sturdy stems.

Senecio longilobus
sen-NEE-shee-oh long-gee-LOW-bus

Yellow blooms of threadleaf mature to silvery seed heads in winter.

THREADLEAF, SILVER GROUNDSEL

- Yellow flowers with golden centers
- Perennial
- Warm and cold deserts
- Zones 4 to 8

Threadleaf is an upright perennial that grows 1 to 3 feet tall and wide. Green leaves are deeply divided, almost threadlike, and covered with fine, silvery-white, woolly hairs. Flowers are yellow with gold centers and bloom in late summer.

USE: This plant performs well in prairie gardens or clustered in large groups in dryland perennial borders. Interplant with fine-textured ornamental grasses, or use them in silver theme gardens.

CULTURE: Threadleaf grows naturally in warm and cold deserts and the Great Plains, in dry, sandy, or gravelly sites, in desert scrub, sand prairie, and piñon-juniper woodlands, at elevations from 2,500 to 7,500 feet. It grows well in most sunny, well-drained sites with pH 7 to 8.5. Little water is required once roots are established.

Combine with broom snakeweed, creosote bush, ephedra, juniper, globe mallow, mountain mahogany, piñon pine, rabbit brush, serviceberry, and three-leaf sumac.

RELATED SPECIES: *Senecio spartioides*, broom groundsel, has green leaves instead of silver. They are deeply divided, 2 to 3 inches long. The plant grows up to 3 feet tall and is covered with numerous yellow ray flowers surrounding a golden center in late summer. The contrast against the green foliage is brilliant.

Sphaeralcea coccinea
sfeer-AL-see-uh cock-SIN-ee-a

Blooming scarlet globe mallow grows at the Pawnee National Grasslands, Colorado.

SCARLET GLOBE MALLOW, COWBOY'S DELIGHT

- Light pink, orange-red, to red flowers
- Perennial
- Warm and cold deserts
- Zones 4 to 8

This is a perennial plant that grows 6 to 10 inches tall. Leaves are grayish-green and deeply lobed. Flowers are light pink to salmon to brick red.

USE: Scarlet globe mallow is a good choice for dryland prairie or rock gardens. It serves well as a low border plant or when combined with cacti and other succulents.

CULTURE: Its natural range is wide, from warm and cold deserts to the Great Plains; on dry sites in chaparral, desert and sage shrublands; in desert and plains grassland and open woodland communities, at elevations from 3,500 to 9,000 feet. Grow it on sunny sites in sand or clay soil. It is tolerant of soils high in gypsum and lime, caliche soil, and soil pH 6 to 8.5. Plants require 10 to 15 inches of rain or irrigation annually, dropping leaves when drought stress is greatest. Viable seeds are produced when moisture is available; more often the plant propagates itself via short, underground stems. It is slow growing, and fertilizers have little effect. Because they develop a substantial taproot, plants are difficult to transplant successfully once established.

Plants combine well with a variety of silver or gray foliage plants. Examples include blackfoot daisy, blue gramagrass, broom snakeweed, buffalograss, desert zinnia, gambel oak, Indian paintbrush, juniper, penstemon species, piñon pine, rabbit brush, sagebrush species, and serviceberry.

FERN VERBENA

Verbena bipinnatifida
ver-BEE-nuh by-pin-nuh-TIF-id-uh

- Pink to lavender flowers
- Spreading perennial
- Warm and cold deserts
- Zones 4 to 8

Fern verbena is a short-lived, sprawling perennial 1 foot tall by 1½ feet wide. Dark green leaves are finely divided, soft, and hairy; stems are wiry. Pink to lavender flowers come in clusters above foliage in spring; bloom extends into summer, when additional moisture is available. It will usually bloom its first year in the garden.

USE: It is excellent in rock gardens, for bedding display, and in perennial borders. Lacy, fine-textured foliage is effective in mass plantings.

CULTURE: This plant grows naturally in warm and cold deserts, in the Great Plains, on sandy to gravelly slopes, along roadsides, and in sparse grasslands, at elevations from 5,000 to 10,000 feet. Plant in full sun to part shade in well-drained soil, pH 6.5 to 8. Water regularly in hot weather. Allow the soil surface to dry between applications. Remove spent blooms to promote flowering. Fern verbena reseeds in sandy and gravelly soil, not in clay.

Combine with blackfoot daisy, fringed sage, Mexican hat coneflower, phlox penstemon, scarlet globe mallow, sundrops, white-tufted evening primrose, and winecup.

RECOMMENDED VARIETIES AND RELATED SPECIES: *Verbena canadensis*, Great Plains verbena, is a trailing plant with trailing purple flowers. Unlike fern verbena, leaves are not lobed. 'Homestead Purple' is a hybrid between *V. canadensis* and an unknown verbena. It blooms for a long time, requires very little maintenance, and needs very little water.

Fern verbena makes a noteworthy companion in a desert garden.

PRAIRIE ZINNIA, DESERT ZINNIA

Zinnia grandiflora
ZIN-ee-a gran-di-FLO-ra

- Yellow flowers with orange centers
- Perennial
- Desert shrub and grasslands
- Zones 5 to 8

Prairie zinnia is a perennial—sometimes annual—mounded plant, 6 to 10 inches tall and wide. Its leaves are small, light green, and needlelike, almost tufted-grassy in appearance. Very long-lasting flowers are golden yellow with orange centers.

USE: This plant excels in dryland perennial borders, prairie or rock gardens, as a low border plant and groundcover, and in annual bedding displays.

CULTURE: It grows naturally in desert shrub and grassland communities in cold and warm deserts and the Great Plains, on dry mesas, hills, and plains, at elevations from 3,000 to 7,000 feet. Grow in full sun in well-drained soils that are high in calcium. Plants tolerate reflected heat and survive with rainfall or irrigation in the 8- to 12-inch range. Plants do not sustain themselves in poorly drained or wet soil, and do not transplant well after they become established.

In gardens, combine prairie zinnia with blackfoot daisy, ephedra, fern verbena, fringed sage, flameflower, pineleaf penstemon, purple groundcherry, scarlet globe mallow, and Utah penstemon.

RELATED SPECIES: *Zinnia acerosa*, white desert zinnia, produces smaller white flowers. It is native to warm deserts, along slopes and flats in limestone soil, and is very drought tolerant.

Light green, narrow leaves and bright yellow flowers of prairie zinnia provide a lively display throughout summer.

USDA Plant Hardiness Zone Map

This map of climate zones helps you select plants for your garden that will survive a typical winter in your region. The United States Department of Agriculture (USDA) developed the map, basing the zones on the lowest recorded temperatures across North America. Zone 1 is the coldest area and Zone 11 is the warmest.

Plants are classified by the coldest temperature and zone they can endure. For example, plants hardy to Zone 6 survive where winter temperatures drop to –10° F. Those hardy to Zone 8 die long before it's that cold. These plants may grow in colder regions but must be replaced each year. Plants rated for a range of hardiness zones can usually survive winter in the coldest region as well as tolerate the summer heat of the warmest one.

To find your hardiness zone, note the approximate location of your community on the map, then match the color band marking that area to the key. Remember that hardiness zones are only a rough guide to plant success.

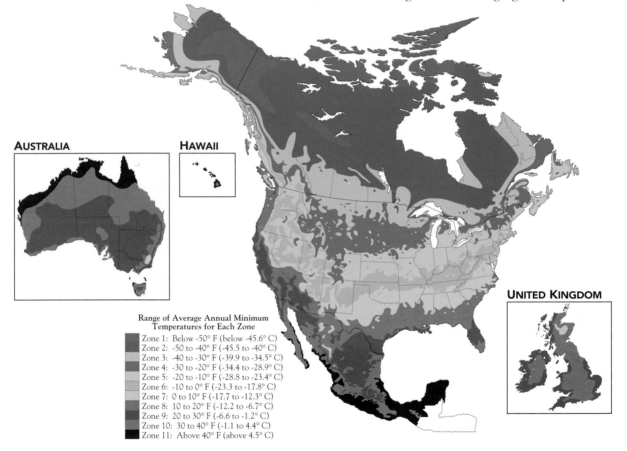

AUSTRALIA

HAWAII

UNITED KINGDOM

Range of Average Annual Minimum Temperatures for Each Zone

Zone 1: Below -50° F (below -45.6° C)
Zone 2: -50 to -40° F (-45.5 to -40° C)
Zone 3: -40 to -30° F (-39.9 to -34.5° C)
Zone 4: -30 to -20° F (-34.4 to -28.9° C)
Zone 5: -20 to -10° F (-28.8 to -23.4° C)
Zone 6: -10 to 0° F (-23.3 to -17.8° C)
Zone 7: 0 to 10° F (-17.7 to -12.3° C)
Zone 8: 10 to 20° F (-12.2 to -6.7° C)
Zone 9: 20 to 30° F (-6.6 to -1.2° C)
Zone 10: 30 to 40° F (-1.1 to 4.4° C)
Zone 11: Above 40° F (above 4.5° C)

METRIC CONVERSIONS

U.S. Units to Metric Equivalents			Metric Units to U.S. Equivalents		
To Convert From	**Multiply By**	**To Get**	**To Convert From**	**Multiply By**	**To Get**
Inches	25.4	Millimeters	Millimeters	0.0394	Inches
Inches	2.54	Centimeters	Centimeters	0.3937	Inches
Feet	30.48	Centimeters	Centimeters	0.0328	Feet
Feet	0.3048	Meters	Meters	3.2808	Feet
Yards	0.9144	Meters	Meters	1.0936	Yards

To convert from degrees Fahrenheit (F) to degrees Celsius (C), first subtract 32, then multiply by ⅝.

To convert from degrees Celsius to degrees Fahrenheit, multiply by ⅝, then add 32.

Resources

Mail-order sources of drought-tolerant plants

Applewood Seed Co.
5380 Vivian St.
Arvada, CO 80002-1921
Info@applewoodseed.com

Bamert Seed Co.
1897 County Rd. 1018
Muleshoe, TX 79347
800/262-9892
www.bamertseed.com

Forestfarm
990 Tetherow Rd.
Williams, OR 97544-9599
541/846-7269
www.forestfarm.com

Great Basin Natives
P.O. Box 114
Holden, UT 84636
435/795-2303
www.greatbasinnatives.com

High Country Gardens
2902 Rufina St.
Santa Fe, NM 87507-2929
800/925-9387
www.highcountrygardens.com

Ion Exchange
1878 Old Mission Dr.
Harpers Ferry, IA 52146-7533
800/291-2143
www.ionxchange.com

Johnston Seed Co.
P.O. Box 1392
Enid, OK 73702
800/375-4613
www.johnstonseed.com

Landscape Alternatives, Inc.
1705 St. Albans St.
Roseville, MN 55113-6554
651/488-3142
landscapealternatives.com
Catalog $2

Larner Seeds
P.O. Box 407
Bolinas, CA 94924
415/868-9407
www.larnerseeds.com
Catalog $2.50

Morning Sky Greenery
24774 450th Ave.
Hancock, MN 56244
320/392-5282
www.morningskygreenery
.com
Catalog $2

Native Seeds/SEARCH
926 N. 4th Ave.
Tucson, AZ 85705
520/622-5561
www.nativeseeds.org
Catalog $1

Plants of the Southwest
3095 Agua Fria
Santa Fe, NM 87507
800/788-7333
www.plantsofthesouthwest
.com
Catalog $3.50

Prairie Habitats, Inc.
Box 10
Argyle, Manitoba R0C 0B0
Canada
204/467-9371
www.prairiehabitats.com
Catalog $2

Prairie Moon Nursery
Rt. 3, Box 1633
Winona, MN 55987
507/452-1362
www.prairiemoonnursery.com

Prairie Nursery, Inc.
P.O. Box 306
Westfield, WI 53964
800/476-9453
www.prairienursery.com

Prairie Restorations, Inc.
P.O. Box 327
Princeton, MN 55371
763/389-4342
www.prairieresto.com

Prairie Ridge Nursery
9738 Overland Rd.
Mt. Horeb, WI 53572-2832
608/437-5245
www.prairieridgenursery.com

Siskiyou Rare Plant Nursery
2825 Cummings Rd.
Medford, Oregon 97501
541/772-6846
siskiyourareplantnursery.com

Sharp Bros. Seed Co., Inc.
104 E. 4th St. Rd.
Greeley, CO 86631
970/356-4710
www.sharpseed.com

Stock Seed Farms, Inc.
28008 Mill Rd.
Murdock, NE 68407-2350
800/759-1520
www.stockseed.com

Taylor Creek Restoration
  Nurseries
17921 Smith Rd.
Brodhead, WI 53520
608/897-8641
www.appliedeco.com/tcrn

Western Native Seed
P.O. Box 188
Coaldale, CO 81222
719/942-3935
http://westernnativeseed.com

Wildflower Farm, Inc.
RR 3
Schomberg, Ontario L0G 1T0
Canada
905/859-0286
www.wildflowerfarm.com

Wild Seed, Inc.
P.O. Box 27751
Tempe, AZ 85042-4718
602/276-3536

Wildseed Farms
425 Wildflower Hills
Fredericksburg, TX 78624-3000
800/848-0078
www.wildseedfarms.com

Index

Page numbers in **bold** indicate illustrations.

A

Acacia constricta, 85, **85**
Acacia cultriformis, **85**
Acacia greggii, 85
Acacia wrightii, 61
Acer grandidentatum, 85, **85**
Achillea (Yarrow), **54**, 55, **83**
Achillea filipendulina, 83
Achillea lanulosa, 108, **108**
Adapted plants, 12–13, 35, 36, 51
Aesculus californica, 86, **86**
Agarita (*Mahonia trifoliata*), 105, **105**
Agastache aurantiaca, 62
Agastache 'Desert Sunrise', 83
Agave (*Agave*), 68, 82
Agave havardiana, 61
Agave lechuguilla, 96, **96**
Algerita (*Mahonia trifoliata*), 105, **105**
Alkali (sodic) soil, 30
Allium, **83**
Aloe (*Aloe*), **37**, **60**, 68, **69**
Amelanchier alnifolia, 96, **96**
American plum (*Prunus americana*), **11**
Amorpha canescens, 97, **97**
Anaphalis triplinervis, 63, **83**
Anethum graveolens, 80
Antennaria dioica, 19, 62, **108**
Antennaria parvifolia, 108
Apache plume (*Fallugia paradoxa*), 102, **102**
Aphids, 48, **48**
Arctostaphylos patula, 97, **97**
Arctostaphylos pungens, 97
Arctostaphylos spp., 68
Arid environments
  plant adaptations to, 12
  types of, 5–11, 29
Arizona cypress (*Cupressus arizonica*), 61, 88, **88**
Arizona fuchsia (*Epilobium canum latifolium*), 112
Arrhenatherum bulbosum, 67
Arroyo lupine (*Lupinus succulentus*), 83
Artemisia, **63**
Artemisia cana, 98
Artemisia dracunculus, 80
Artemisia filifolia, 60
Artemisia frigida, 62, 75, 109, **109**
Artemisia ludoviciana, 109
Artemisia millefolium, 108
Artemisia stelleriana, 62, **82**
Artemisia tridentata, 60, 98, **98**
Artemisia versicolor, 62
Artemisia 'Powis Castle,' 83
Asclepias tuberosa, 109, **109**

Ash, singleleaf (*Fraxinus anomala*), 89, **89**
Ash, velvet (*Fraxinus velutina*), 89
Astragalus spp., 75
Atriplex canescens, 60, 98, **98**

B

Baileya multiradiata, 110, **110**
Banana yucca (*Yucca baccata*), 61
Barberry, red (*Berberis haematocarpa*), **105**
Bark mulch, 45, **76**
Barren strawberry (*Waldsteinia ternata*), 55
Beach wormwood (*Artemisia stelleriana*), 62, **82**
Beavertail cactus (*Opuntia basilaris*), **68**
Beneficial insects, 48
Berberis haematocarpa, **105**
Berberis trifoliata, 105, **105**
Berlandiera lyrata, 110, **110**
Big sagebrush (*Artemisia tridentata*), 60, 98, **98**
Bigtooth maple (*Acer grandidentatum*), 85, **85**
Birchleaf mountain mahogany (*Cercocarpus betuloides*), 88
Black eyed Susan (*Rudbeckia hirta*), **9**, **66**, 119, **119**
Blackfoot daisy (*Melampodium leucanthum*), 83, 115, **115**
Blanket flower (*Gaillardia* spp.), 75, 114, **114**
Blue avena (*Helictotrichon sempervirens*), 63, 67
Blue fescue (*Festuca cinerea*), 67
Blue fescue (*Festuca glauca*), 63
Blue gardens, 61–63
Blue gramagrass (*Bouteloua gracilis*), **52**, 55, 75
Blue hair grass (*Koeleria glauca*), 67
Blue lyme grass (*Elymus glaucus*), 63
Blue oak (*Quercus douglasii*), 92
Blue palo verde (*Cercidium floridum*), 87, **87**
Blue spruce sedum (*Sedum reflexum*), 63
Bluestem, little (*Schizachyrium scoparium*), 61, 65, 75
Bouteloua curtipendula, 75
Bouteloua gracilis. See Blue gramagrass
Brittle bush (*Encelia*), 68
Briza media, 67
Broom groundsel (*Senecio spartioides*), 120
Broom snakeweed (*Gutierrezia sarothrae*), 75, 114, **114**
Bubbler irrigation, 40–41
Buckeye, California (*Aesculus californica*), 86, **86**
Buckthorn, sea (*Hippophae rhamnoides*), 60, **84**
Buckwheat, **5**, 113, **113**
Buddleia alternifolia, 60
Buffaloberry (*Shepherdia*), 62, **84**
Buffalograss (*Buchloe dactyloides*), 55, **55**, 75
Bulbous oatgrass (*Arrhenatherum bulbosum*), 67
Burro's tail (*Sedum morganianum*), 63
Bush morning glory (*Ipomoea leptophylla*), 115, **115**
Butterfly weed (*Asclepias tuberosa*), 109, **109**
Butterflybush, silver (*Buddleia alternifolia*), 60

C

Cactus, **21**, 68, **68**, 69, 75
Calamagrostis spp., **4**, 67
Caliche, 29
California buckeye (*Aesculus californica*), 86, **86**
California buckwheat (*Eriogonum fasciculatum foliosum*), 113, **113**
California fan palm (*Washingtonia filifera*), 95, **95**
California fuchsia (*Epilobium canum canum*), 112, **112**
California gold poppy (*Eschscholzia californica*), **74**, 83
Callirhoe involucrata, 83
Canterbury bells, desert (*Phacelia campanularia*), 83
Cape blanco sedum (*Sedum spathulifolium*), 63
Catclaw acacia (*Acacia greggii*), 85
Ceanothus greggii, 99, **99**
Celtis reticulata, 86, **86**
Centranthus, **22**
Cephalocereus senilis, 68
Cerastium tomentosum, 62
Cercidium floridum, 87, **87**
Cercidium microphylum, 61
Cercis occidentalis, 87, **87**
Cercocarpus betuloides, 88
Cercocarpus ledifolius, 88, **88**
Chamaebatiaria millefolium, 99, **99**
Chaparral, 10
Chihuahuan desert, 6–8
Chilopsis linearis, 100, **100**
Chisos agave (*Agave hardiniana*), 61
Chocolate flower (*Berlandiera lyrata*), 110, **110**
Cholla (*Opuntia* spp.), 69
Chrysothamnus nauseosus, 100
Chrysothamnus viscidiflorus, 100, **100**
Cilantro (*Coriandrum sativum*), 80
Clarkia, **74**
Clay soils, 26–27, 32
Cleome lutea, 83
Cliffrose (*Cowania mexicana stansburiana*), 101, **101**
Clover, hairy canary (*Dorycnium hirsutum*), 62
Clover, purple prairie (*Dalea purpurea*), **9**, 75, 111, **111**
Coast live oak (*Quercus agrifolia*), 92, **92**
Cold deserts, 8–9
Columbine, **53**
Common sage (*Salvia officinalis*), 80, 81
Common yarrow (*Artemisia millefolium*), 108
Composting, 23, 42–44, 59, 78
Conservation, 4–5
  microclimates and, 20–23
  of nutrients, 23, 42–44, 59, 78
  of water, 20–23, 36–39, 56–58
Cool season grasses, 66–67
Coreopsis tinctoria, 83

Coriander (*Coriandrum sativum*), 80
Cortaderia selloana. See Pampas grass
Cover crops, 31
Cowania mexicana stansburiana, 101, **101**
Cowboy's delight. *See* Scarlet globemallow
Creeping hollygrape (*Mahonia repens*), 55, 106, **106**
Creeping juniper (*Juniperus horizontalis*), 55, 61
Creeping speedwell (*Veronica* 'Blue Reflection'), 83
Creeping thyme (*Thymus*), **5**, **81**
Creeping zinnia (*Sanvitalia procumbens*), 83
Crocus, **21**
Crown rot, 37
Cumin (*Cuminum cuminum*), 80
Cupleaf ceanothus (*Ceanothus greggii*), 99, **99**
Cupressus arizonica, 61, 88, **88**
Cupressus glabra, 88
Curlicue sage (*Artemisia versicolor*), 62
Curlleaf mountain mahogany (*Cercocarpus ledifolius*), 88, **88**
Curry plant (*Helichrysum angustifolium*), 81
Cutleaf fleabane (*Erigeron compositus*), 112, **112**
Cypress, Arizona (*Cupressus arizonica*), 61, 88, **88**
Cypress, smooth (*Cupressus glabra*), 88

D

Dalea greggii, 111, **111**
Dalea purpurea, **9**, 75, 111, **111**
Dasylirion, 68
Delphinium, **53**
Desert canterbury bells (*Phacelia campanularia*), 83
Desert ceanothus (*Ceanothus greggii*), 99, **99**
Desert four o'clock (*Mirabilis multiflora*), 116, **116**
Desert marigold (*Baileya multiradiata*), 110, **110**
Desert spoon (*Dasylirion*), 68
Desert willow (*Chilopsis linearis*), 100, **100**
Desert zinnia (*Zinnia grandiflora*), 83, 121, **121**
Deserts, 6–9
Dill (*Anethum graveolens*), 80
Diplacus longiflorus (*Mimulus longiflorus*), 116, **116**
Disease management, 48–49
Diversity in plantings, 54
Dodonaea viscosa, 101, **101**
Dorycnium hirsutum, 62
Dotted gayfeather (*Liatris punctata*), 75
Drainage, 29, 32, 37
Drip irrigation, 40
Dropseed, sand (*Sporobolus cryptandrus*), 75
Dusty miller (*Senecio cineraria*), 62, **81**, 82, 83

E

Echeveria (*Echeveria* spp.), 63
Echeveria setosa, **62**
Echinacea purpura, **4**, **9**
Echinocereus pectinatus, 68
Elaeagnus commutata, 60

Elymus arenarius, 65
Elymus glaucus, 63
Elymus magellanicus, 65
Encelia farinosa, 111, **111**
Encelia spp., 68
Ephedra (*Ephedra* spp.), 68
Ephedra viridis, 102, **102**
Epilobium canum canum, 112, **112**
Epilobium canum latifolium, 112
Erianthus ravennae, 65
Erigeron caespitosa, 112
Erigeron compositus, 112, **112**
Eriogonum fasciculatum foliosum, 113, **113**
Eriogonum umbellatum, 113, **113**
Erysimum, **53**
Evapotranspiration (ET), 58
Evening primrose (*Oenothera* spp.), **52**, 83, 117, **117**
Everlasting (*Anaphalis*), **63**, **83**
Exotic plants, 12–14, 36, 49, 51, 71, 72

F

Fabric mulch, 47, **78**
Fallugia paradoxa, 102, **102**
Feather grass, Mexican (*Nassella tenuissima*), 65
Feather reed grass (*Calamagrostis* spp.), **4**, 67
Fern verbena (*Verbena bipinnatifida*), 121, **121**
Fernbush (*Chamaebatiaria millefolium*), 99, **99**
Ferocactus wislizenii, 69
Fertilizers, 5, 42
Festuca amethystina, 67
Festuca glauca, 63, 67
Festuca idahoensis, 61
Fibrous rooted plants, 37, 40, 53
Fishhook cactus (*Ferocactus wislizeni*), 69
Flannel bush (*Fremontodendron californicum*), 103, **103**
Fleabane (*Erigeron compositus*), 112, **112**
Forestiera neomexicana, 103, **103**
Fountain grass (*Pennisetum* spp.), 65, **66**, 83
Fouquieria splendens, 69, 104, **104**
Four o'clock (*Mirabilis*), 83, 116, **116**
Four-wing saltbush (*Atriplex canescens*), 60, 98, **98**
Fraxinus anomala, 89, **89**
Fraxinus velutina, 89
Fremont mahonia (*Mahonia fremontii*), 105
Fremontodendron californicum, 103, **103**
French tarragon (*Artemisia dracunculus*), 80
Fringed sage (*Artemisia frigida*), 62, 75, 109, **109**
Fuchsia (*Epilobium*), 82, 112, **112**

G

Gaillardia aristata, 75, 114
Gaillardia pinnatifida, 114, **114**
Gaillardia pulchella, 83
Galeta grass (*Hilaria jamesii*), 75

Gambel oak (*Quercus gambelii*), 93, **93**
Gayfeather, dotted (*Liatris punctata*), 75
Gazania (*Gazania rigens*), 83
Giant four o'clock (*Mirabilis multiflora*), 116, **116**
Globe amaranth (*Gomphrena globosa*), 83
Globemallow, scarlet (*Sphaeralcea coccinea*), 75, 120, **120**
Gloriosa daisy (*Rudbeckia hirta*), 83
Gomphrena globosa, 83
Gramagrass (*Bouteloua*), 55, **55**, 75
Grasses. *See* Lawns; Ornamental grass gardens
Grasslands, 9
Great Basin, 8–9
Great plains verbena (*Verbena canadensis*), 121
Greek oregano (*Origanum heracleoticum*), 80
Green ephedra (*Ephedra viridis*), 102, **102**
Green rabbitbrush (*Chrysothamnus viscidiflorus*), 100, **100**
Greenleaf manzanita (*Arctostaphylos patula*), 97, **97**
Groundcovers, 39, 55, 80–81
Groundsel (*Senecio*), 75, 120, **120**
Growing seasons, 52
Growth rate of plants, 21, 36, 53
Gutierrezia sarothrae, 75, 114, **114**

H

Hackberry, netleaf (*Celtis reticulata*), 86, **86**
Hairy canary clover (*Dorycnium hirsutum*), 62
Hand watering, 40
Hardiness zones, 84
Hardpans, 29, 35
Harestail grass (*Lagurus ovatus*), 65
Helianthemum, **22**
Helianthus spp., 75
Helichrysum italicum, 81
Helichrysum petiolare, 62
Helictotrichon sempervirens, 63, 67
Herb gardens, 80–81
Herbicides, 49
Hesperaloe parviflora, 83
High pressure irrigation systems, 40
Hilaria jamesii, 75
Hippophae rhamnoides, 60, **84**
Holcus mollis, 67
Hollygrape, creeping (*Mahonia repens*), 55, 106, **106**
Hopbush (*Dodonaea viscosa*), 101, **101**
Horizontal juniper (*Juniperus horizontalis*), 55, 61
Hummingbird plant (*Zauschneria garrettii*), 83, 112
Hummingbird trumpet (*Epilobium canum canum*), 112, **112**
Hydromulching, **73**
Hydrozones, 39
Hyssop (*Agastache aurantiaca*), 62

I

Incienso (*Encelia farinosa*), 111, **111**
Indian blanket (*Gaillardia pulchella*), 83
Indian grass (*Sorghastrum nutans*), 65
Indigo bush, trailing (*Dalea greggii*), 111, **111**
Inorganic fertilizer, 42
Insect pests, 48
Insecticides, 5, 48
Integrated Pest Management (IPM), 49
Interior live oak (*Quercus wislizeni*), 92
Introduced plants. *See* Exotic plants
Ipomoea leptophylla, 115, **115**
Iris, **33**, **53**, **56**
Iron, 42
Irrigation, 20–21, 38–39, 40–41, 77
Irrigation systems, 40–41
Italian parsley (*Petroselinum crispum*), 80

J

Jeffrey pine (*Pinus jeffreyi*), 91
Jerusalem thorn (*Parkinsonia aculeata*), 90, **90**
Jojoba (*Simmondsia chinensis*), 69
Joshua tree (*Yucca brevifolia*), **8**, 95, **95**
June grass (*Koeleria cristata*), 75
Juniper. *See Juniperus*
Juniperus horizontalis, 55, 61
Juniperus monosperma, 89, **89**
Juniperus osteosperma, 89, **89**
Jupiter's beard (*Centranthus*), **22**

K

Kentucky bluegrass, **53**
Knife acacia (*Acacia cultriformis*), **85**
Kniphofia uvaria, 83
Koeleria cristata, 75
Koeleria glauca, 67

L

Lady bugs, 48, **48**
Lagurus ovatus, 65
Lamb's-ears (*Stachys byzantina*), 62, **62**
Large flowered penstemon (*Penstemon grandiflorus*), 118, **118**
Laurus nobilis, 80, 81
Lavender (*Lavandula* spp.), **54**, 62, 81
Lawns, 21–22, 54–56
Leadplant, silver (*Amorpha canescens*), 97, **97**
Lechuguilla (*Agave lechuguilla*), 96, **96**
Lemon balm (*Melissa officinalis*), 80, 81
Leucophyllum frutescens, 60, **60**, 104, **104**
Liatris 'Alba,' **4**
Liatris punctata, 75
Licorice plant (*Helichrysum petiolare*), 62
Lithops spp., 69
Little bluestem (*Schizachyrium scoparium*), 61, 65, 75

Littleleaf palo verde (*Cercidium microphyllum*), 87
Littleleaf pussy-toes (*Antennaria parvifolia*), 108, **108**
Littleleaf sumac (*Rhus microphylla*), 107, **107**
Live oak
    coast (*Quercus agrifolia*), 92, **92**
    interior (*Quercus wislizeni*), 92
    shrub (*Quercus turbinella*), 106, **106**
Living stones (*Lithops* spp.), 69
Loam, 24–25, 27
Locoweed (*Astragalus* spp.), 75
Locoweed (*Oxytropis lambertii*), 75
Locust, New Mexico (*Robinia neomexicana*), 107, **107**
Loosestrife, purple, 49
Low pressure irrigation systems, 40–41
Lupine, arroyo (*Lupinus succulentus*), 83
Lyme grass (*Elymus arenarius, E. magellanicus*), 65
Lyme grass, blue (*Elymus glaucus*), 63

M

Mahogany, birchleaf mountain (*Cercocarpus betuloides*), 88
Mahogany, curlleaf (*Cercocarpus ledifolius*), 88, **88**
Mahonia fremontii, 105
Mahonia repens, 55, 106, **106**
Mahonia trifoliata, 105, **105**
Maiden grass (*Miscanthus oligostachys, M. sinensis*), 65
Manure, 31
Manzanita (*Arctostaphylos* spp.), 68, 97, **97**
Maple, bigtooth (*Acer grandidentatum*), 85, **85**
Marigold, desert (*Baileya multiradiata*), 110, **110**
Marigold (*Tagetes* spp.), 83
Marjoram, sweet (*Origanum majorana*), 80
Mealycup sage (*Salvia farinacea*), **82**, 83
Melampodium leucanthum, 83, 115, **115**
Melissa officinalis, 80, 81
Mentha spp., **5**, 80
Mescal bean (*Sophora secundiflora*), 94, **94**
Mesquite (*Prosopis* spp.), 92, **92**
Mexican evening primrose (*Oenothera mexicana*), **52**
Mexican feather grass (*Nassella tenuissima*), 65
Mexican hat coneflower (*Ratibida columnifera*), 75, 119, **119**
Mexican sunflower (*Tithonia rotundifolia*), 83
Micro irrigation systems, 40–41
Micro spray irrigation, 40
Microclimates
    conservation and, 20–23
    plant selection and, 21–22, 84
    types of, 16–19
Microorganisms, 32, 43–44
Mimulus longiflorus, 116

Mint (*Mentha* spp.), **5**, 80
Mirabilis jalapa, 83, 116
Mirabilis multiflora, 116, **116**
Miscanthus oligostachys, 65
Miscanthus sinensis, 65
Mohave desert, 8
Monkey flower, southern bush (*Mimulus longiflorus*), 116, **116**
Morning glory, bush (*Ipomoea leptophylla*), 115, **115**
Moss rose (*Portulaca grandiflora*), 83
Moss verbena (*Verbena tenuisecta*), **68**
Mulches, 39, 45–47, **73**, **78**
Mycorrhizae, 32

N

Narrowleaf zinnia (*Zinnia angustifolia*), 83
Nassella tenuissima, 65
Natal grass (*Rhynchelytrum repens*), 65
Native plants, 12–13, 35, 36, 51
Needle and thread (*Stipa comata*), 75
Netleaf hackberry (*Celtis reticulata*), 86, **86**
New Mexico locust (*Robinia neomexicana*), 107, **107**
New Mexico privet (*Forestiera neomexicana*), 103, **103**
New Zealand flax, **58**
Nitrogen, 42
Nitrogen fixing plants, 22
Non adapted plants, 14, 36, 51
Non organic mulches, 46–47
Noxious weeds, 49, 71, 72
Nutrients, in soils, 30, 42–44

O

Oak. *See also* Live oak
    blue (*Quercus douglasii*), 92
    Gambel (*Quercus gambelii*), 93, **93**
    turbinella (*Quercus turbinella*), 106, **106**
Ocotillo (*Fouquieria splendens*), 69, 104, **104**
Oenothera caespitosa, 117, **117**
Oenothera macrocarpa, 83
Oenothera macrocarpa, 117
Old man cactus (*Cephalocereus senilis*), 68
One-seed juniper (*Juniperus monosperma*), 89, **89**
Open woodlands, 11
Opuntia basilaris, **68**
Opuntia polyacantha. See Prickly pear cactus
Opuntia spp., 69
Oregano, Greek (*Origanum heracleoticum*), 80
Organic fertilizer, 42
Organic mulches, 45–46
Origanum heracleoticum, 80
Origanum majorana, 80
Ornamental grass gardens, 64–67
Oxytropis lambertii, 75
Ozark sundrop (*Oenothera macrocarpa*), 117

Serviceberry, western (*Amelanchier alnifolia*), 96, **96**
Shady microenvironments, 16, 18
Shepherdia argentea, 62
Shrub live oak (*Quercus turbinella*), 106, **106**
Shrubby cinquefoil, 48
Shrublands, 10
Shrubs, 96–107
Sideoats gramagrass (*Bouteloua curtipendula*), 75
Silver buffaloberry (*Shepherdia argentea*), 62
Silver butterflybush (*Buddleia alternifolia*), 60
Silver gardens, 60–63
Silver groundsel (*Senecio longilobus*), 75, 120, **120**
Silver lead-plant (*Amorpha canescens*), 97, **97**
Silver sage (*Artemisia* 'Powis Castle'), 83
Silver sage (*Salvia argentea*), 62, **63**
Silver sagebrush (*Artemisia cana*), 98
Silver speedwell (*Veronica incana*), 62
Silverberry (*Elaeagnus commutata*), 60
Simmondsia chinensis, 69
Single leaf pine (*Pinus monophylla*), 90
Singleleaf ash (*Fraxinus anomala*), 89, **89**
Site evaluation, 14–15, 52, 84
Slender blanket flower (*Gaillardia pinnatifida*), 114, **114**
Sloping microenvironments, 18
Sludge, as fertilizer, 31
Smooth cypress (*Cupressus glabra*), 88
Snakeweed, broom (*Gutierrezia sarothrae*), 75, 114, **114**
Snow-in-summer (*Cerastium tomentosum*), 62
Soapberry, western (*Sapindus drummondii*), 94, **94**
Sodic (alkali) soil, 30
Soil amendments, 22, 23, 30–32, 42, 78
Soil moisture sensors, 41
Soil pH, 30, 32
Soil profile, 28–29
Soil tests, 32
Soils, 5, 24–32
    alkalinity and salinity, 30
    drainage of, 29, 32, 37
    nutrients in, 30, 42–44
    texture and structure of, 26–28
    types of, 23, 24–28, 30
Sonoran desert, 8
Sophora secundiflora, 94, **94**
Sorghastrum nutans, 65
Southern bush monkey flower (*Mimulus longiflorus*), 116, **116**
Spanish bayonet (*Yucca*), **60**
Speedwell (*Veronica*), 62, 83
Sphaeralcea coccinea, 75, 120, **120**
Spiderflower, yellow (*Cleome lutea*), 83
Spiderwort, prairie (*Tradescantia occidentalis*), 75
Spiny saltbush (*Atriplex confertifolia*), 60

Stachys byzantina, 62, **62**
Stipa comata, 75
Subsoil irrigation systems, 41
Succulent plants, 37, 68–69
Sulfur flower (*Eriogonum umbellatum*), 113, **113**
Sumac, littleleaf (*Rhus microphylla*), 107, **107**
Sumac, three-leaf (*Rhus trilobata*), 107, **107**
Summer savory (*Satureja hortensis*), 80
Sunflower (*Helianthus* spp.), 75
Sunflower, Mexican (*Tithonia rotundifolia*), 83
Sunny microenvironments, 16
Sunrose (*Helianthemum*), **22**
Sweet bay (*Laurus nobilis*), 80, 81
Sweet marjoram (*Origanum majorana*), 80
Switchgrass (*Panicum virgatum*), 63, 65

T

Tagetes spp., 83
Tall sagebrush (*Artemisia tridentata*), 60, 98, **98**
Tamarix (*Tamarix parviflora*), **48**, 49
Tap rooted plants, 37, 40, 53
Tarragon, French (*Artemisia dracunculus*), 80
Texas honey mesquite (*Prosopis glandulosa*), 92, **92**
Texas mountain laurel (*Sophora secundiflora*), 94, **94**
Texas live oak (*Quercus virginiana*), 92
Texas red yucca (*Hesperaloe parviflora*), 83
Texas sage (*Leucophyllum frutescens*), 60, **60**, 104, **104**
Thornscrub, 10–11
Threadleaf (*Senecio longilobus*), 120, **120**
Three-leaf sumac (*Rhus trilobata*), 107, **107**
Thyme (*Thymus* spp.), **5**, 19, 80, **81**
Tickseed (*Coreopsis tinctoria*), 83
Tithonia rotundifolia, 83
Tradescantia occidentalis, 75
Trailing indigo bush (*Dalea greggii*), 111, **111**
Transplanting, 33–35
Tree bark mulch, 45
Trees, 85–95
Tufted fescue (*Festuca amethystina*), 67
Tufted fleabane (*Erigeron caespitosa*), 112
Turbinella oak (*Quercus turbinella*), 106, **106**
Two needle piñon pine (*Pinus edulis*), 90, **90**

U

Utah juniper (*Juniperus osteosperma*), 89, **89**

V

Vegetable gardens, 35, 39, 49, 76–79
Velvet ash (*Fraxinus velutina*), 89
Velvet grass (*Holcus mollis*), 67
Velvet mesquite (*Prosopis juliflora*), 92
Verbena bipinnatifida, 121, **121**
Verbena bonariensis, **83**

Verbena canadensis, 121
Verbena tenuisecta, **68**
Veronica incana, 62
Veronica 'Blue Reflection', 83
Victorian gardens, 82–83

W

Waldsteinia ternata, 55
Warm deserts, 6–8
Warm season grasses, 65
Washingtonia filifera, 95, **95**
Water conservation, 20–23, 36–39, 56–58. *See also* Irrigation
Watering zones, 39
Weed management, 49
Western redbud (*Cercis occidentalis*), 87, **87**
Western serviceberry (*Amelanchier alnifolia*), 96, **96**
Western soapberry (*Sapindus drummondii*), 94, **94**
Western wheat (*Pascopyrum smithii*), 75
Western yarrow (*Achillea lanulosa*), 108, **108**
Wheat, western (*Pascopyron smithii*), 75
White desert zinnia (*Zinnia acerosa*), 121
White sage (*Artemisia ludoviciana*), 109
White thorn acacia (*Acacia constricta*), 85, **85**
White tufted evening primrose (*Oenothera caespitosa*), 117, **117**
Willow, desert (*Chilopsis linearis*), 100, **100**
Willow-leaf pear (*Pyrus salicifolia*), 60
Wind sensors, 41
Windy microenvironments, 16–17
Winecup (*Callirhoe involucrata*), 83
Wood mulch, 45
Woolly paper flower (*Psilostrophe tagetina*), 118, **118**
Wormwood (*Artemisia*), **53**, 62, **82**
Wright acacia (*Acacia wrightii*), 61

X-Y

Xanthocephalum sarothrae. See Gutierrezia sarothrae
Yarrow (*Achillea*), **54**, 55, 83, **83**, 108, **108**
Yellow buckwheat, **5**
Yellow palo verde, 61
Yellow spider flower (*Cleome lutea*), 83
Yucca baccata, 61
Yucca brevifolia, **8**, 95, **95**
Yucca spp., **60**, 69

Z

Zauschneria californica, 112, **112**
Zauschneria garrettii, 83, 112
Zinnia, creeping (*Sanvitalia procumbens*), 83
Zinnia acerosa, 121
Zinnia angustifolia, 83
Zinnia grandiflora, 83, 121, **121**

P

Palm, California fan *(Washingtonia filifera)*, 95, **95**
Palo verde, **52**
    blue *(Cercidium floridum)*, 61, 87, **87**
    littleleaf *(Cercidium microphyllum)*, 87
Pampas grass *(Cortaderia selloana)*, 49, **49**, 65, 82
Panicum virgatum, 63, 65
Paper flower, woolly *(Psilostrophe*
    tagetina), 118, **118**
Parkinsonia aculeata, 90, **90**
Parklands, 11
Parsley, Italian *(Petroselinum crispum)*, 80
Pascopyrum smithii, 75
Paved areas, 18–19, 56–57
Pear, willow-leaf *(Pyrus salicifolia)*, 60
Pearly everlasting *(Anaphalis triplinervis)*, **63**, **83**
Pennisetum spp., 65, **66**, 83
Penstemon ambiguus, 117, **117**
Penstemon grandiflorus, 118, **118**
Penstemon pinifolius. See Pineleaf penstemon
Perennials, 34, 108–121
Perovskia atriplicifolia, 62
Pest management, 48–49
Pesticides, 5, 48, 49
Petalostemon purpureum. See Purple
    prairie clover
Petroselinum neapolitanum, 80
Petunia *(Petunia* hybrids), 83
Phacelia campanularia, 83
Phalaris arundinacea, 67
Phlox penstemon *(Penstemon ambiguus)*,
    117, **117**
Phosphorus, 42
Pine
    Jeffrey *(Pinus jeffreyi)*, 91
    piñon *(Pinus edulis)*, 48, **84**, 90, **90**
    ponderosa *(Pinus ponderosa)*, 91, **91**
    single leaf *(Pinus monophylla)*, 90
Pine needle mulch, 45
Pineleaf penstemon *(Penstemon pinifolius)*,
    5, 118, **118**
Piñon pine *(Pinus)*, 48, **84**, 90, **90**
Pinus edulis, 90, **90**
Pinus jeffereyi, 91
Pinus monophylla, 90
Pinus ponderosa, 91, **91**
Planning, 51–55
Plant selection
    for arid gardens, 12–13, 51–54
    microclimates and, 21–22, 84
    for prairie gardens, 71–72, 75
Planting, 33–35, 72–73
Plastic mulch, 47
Plum, American *(Prunus americana)*, **11**
Ponderosa pine *(Pinus ponderosa)*, 91, **91**
Portulaca grandiflora, 83
Potassium, 42

Prairie coneflower. *See* Mexican hat coneflower
Prairie gardens, 70–75
Prairie spiderwort *(Tradescantia occidentalis)*, 75
Prairie zinnia. *See* Desert zinnia
Prairies, 9, 29
Prickly pear cactus *(Opuntia polyacantha)*,
    21, 69, 75
Privet, New Mexico *(Forestiera*
    neomexicana), 103, **103**
Prosopis glandulosa, 92, **92**
Prosopis juliflora, 92
Prunus americana, **11**
Psilostrophe tagetina, 118, **118**
Purple coneflower. *See Echinacea purpura*
Purple loosestrife, 49
Purple prairie clover *(Dalea purpurea)*, **9**,
    75, 111, **111**
Purpletop verbena *(Verbena bonariensis)*, **83**
Pussy-toes *(Antennaria dioica)*, 19, 62, **108**
Pussy-toes, littleleaf *(Antennaria*
    parvifolia), 108, **108**
Pyrus salicifolia, 60

Q

Quaking grass *(Briza media)*, 67
Quercus agrifolia, 92, **92**
Quercus douglasii, 92
Quercus gambelii, 93, **93**
Quercus turbinella, 106, **106**
Quercus virginiana, 92
Quercus wislizeni, 92

R

Rabbitbrush *(Chrysothamnus)*, 100, **100**
Rain sensors, 41
Rainwater collection, 23, 56–57. *See also*
    Runoff water
Raised beds, for vegetables, 77, **77**
Ratibida columnifera, 75, 119, **119**
Ravenna grass *(Erianthus ravennae)*, 65
Recycling, 23, 42–43, 59
Red barberry *(Berberis haematocarpa)*, **105**
Red hot poker *(Kniphofia uvaria)*, 83
Redbud, western *(Cercis occidentalis)*, 87, **87**
Rhus microphylla, 107, **107**
Rhus trilobata, 107, **107**
Rhynchelytrum nerviglume, 65
Rhynchelytrum repens, 65
Ribbon grass *(Phalaris arundinacea)*, 67
Robinia neomexicana, 107, **107**
Rock mulch, 47
Roof runoff collection, 23, 56–57
Root bound plants, 33
Root rot, 37
Roots, 33, 37, 52–53
Rosemary *(Rosmarinus officinalis)*, 80, 81, **81**
Rubber rabbitbrush *(Chrysothamnus nauseosus)*, 100

Rubygrass *(Rhynchelytrum nerviglu*
    Rudbeckia, **4**
Rudbeckia hirta, **9**, **66**, 83, 119, **119**
Runoff water, conserving, 23, 56–58
Russet buffaloberry, **84**
Russian olive, 49
Russian sage *(Perovskia atriplicifolia*

S

Sage
    common *(Salvia officinalis)*, 80, 81
    curlicue *(Artemisia versicolor)*, 62
    fringed *(Artemisia frigida)*, 62, 75, 109,
    mealycup *(Salvia farinacea)*, **82**, 83
    Russian *(Perovskia atriplicifolia)*, 62
    sand *(Artemisia filifolia)*, 60
    silver *(Artemisia* 'Powis Castle'), 83
    silver *(Salvia argentea)*, 62, **63**
    Texas *(Leucophyllum frutescens)*, 60,
    104, **104**
    white *(Artemisia ludoviciana)*, 109
Sagebrush *(Artemisia)*, 10, 60, 98, **98**
Saline soils, 30
Salt accumulation, 17, 29
Saltbush, four-wing *(Atriplex canescens)*, 98, **9**
Saltbush, spiny *(Atriplex confertifolia)*, 60
Salvia, **5**, **53**
Salvia argentea, 62, **63**
Salvia farinacea, **82**, 83
Salvia officinalis, 80, 81
Salvia 'Raspberry Delight', 83
Sand dropseed *(Sporobolus cryptandrus)*, 75
Sand sage *(Artemisia filifolia)*, 60
Sandy soil, 26
Santa Barbara daisy *(Erigeron)*, **58**
Santolina, **81**
Sanvitalia procumbens, 83
Sapindus drummondii, 94, **94**
Saskatoon *(Amelanchier alnifolia)*, 96, **96**
Satureja hortensis, 80
Savannas, 11
Savory, summer *(Satureja hortensis)*, 80
Sawdust mulch, 46
Scarlet globemallow *(Sphaeralcea*
    coccinea), 75, 120, **120**
Schizachyrium scoparium, 61, 65, 75
Scrub, 10–11
Sculpture gardens, 68–69
Sea buckthorn *(Hippophae rhamnoides)*, 60, **84**
Sedum morganianum, 63
Sedum reflexum, 63
Sedum spathulifolium, 63
Senecio cineraria. See Dusty miller
Senecio longilobus, 75, 120, **120**
Senecio spartioides, 120
Sensors for irrigation systems, 41